Strategic Studies Institute Book

NATIONAL SECURITY REFORM 2010: A MID-TERM ASSESSMENT

Joseph R. Cerami
Robert H. Dorff
Matthew H. Harber
Editors

August 2011

*****

Published by Books Express Publishing
Books Express, 2011
ISBN 978-1-780395-50-0

Books Express publications are available from all good retail and online booksellers. For
publishing proposals and direct ordering please contact us at: info@books-express.com

IN MEMORIAM
Harvey Sicherman
1945-2010

Harvey Sicherman died quite suddenly on December 25, 2010. Not long before, he had completed the manuscript that now appears as Chapter 6 in this book. He presented the original paper at the April 22, 2010, Symposium in Washington, DC. Testimonials to his life, his accomplishments, and his legacy appeared almost immediately following his death, and include a special issue of *Orbis* published by the Foreign Policy Research Institute where he served as President *(http://www.fpri.org/orbis/5503.html)*. The authors of this edited volume wanted to add to this publication an acknowledgement of what Harvey had meant to so many of us. We thought it most appropriate to ask a colleague from the Strategic Studies Institute who had known him for more than 40 years to share his thoughts.

> I first met Harvey Sicherman in 1967 when he was a graduate student at the University of Pennsylvania. Harvey stood out then for his sartorial splendor in an era of bell bottoms and beards. But it was and remained more than sartorial elegance that drew people to him. It soon became clear that he had a penetrating intelligence, coruscating wit, great charm, and deep passion, a rare combination even then among students of international affairs. When I later encountered him as Secretary of State Haig's assistant, I was not surprised by his rise. Neither could I then or now think of anyone better qualified for the position. As leader of the Foreign Policy Research Institute, Harvey then gave his utmost to restoring FPRI to its previous glory in another sign of his commitment, passion, intelligence, and charm. At the same time he never lost his

profound religious commitment that prevented these gifts from becoming style rather than substance. Harvey may have slaughtered several sacred cows, but he never denied the importance of the sacred in human affairs. He left us all far too soon. May his memory be a blessing.

Stephen J. Blank, Ph.D.
Professor, Strategic Studies Institute
U.S. Army War College
Carlisle, Pa

CONTENTS

FOREWORD

On April 22, 2010, the Bush School of Government and Public Service at Texas A&M University, and the Strategic Studies Institute (SSI), U.S. Army War College, conducted a colloquium in Washington, DC, on "2010: Preparing for a Mid-Term Assessment of Leadership and National Security Reform in the Obama Administration." This conference marked the fifth collaboration between the Bush School and SSI. The first, "The Future of Transatlantic Security Relations," was held in 2006. In 2007, a workshop was held in College Station, Texas, on "The Interagency and Counterinsurgency Warfare." The third conference, "Reform and the Next President's Agenda," was held in March 2008, also in College Station, Texas. That conference was also co-sponsored by the nonpartisan Project on National Security Reform (PNSR), which includes retired Lieutenant General Brent Scowcroft as a member of its Guiding Coalition. The PNSR guiding coalition also originally included several key members of the Obama administration. The fourth conference, "Leadership and Government Reform," took place in June 2009. Two major topics were discussed: leader development in professional schools and leadership and "whole of government" reforms.

The theme of the 2010 colloquium continued the discussion of "whole of government" reforms, but added three new areas of emphasis. The first identified the critical need for congressional leadership in carrying out transformational national security reforms. The second addressed improving methods of strategic planning and assessment to meet the current U.S. fiscal constraints. The third discussed the transition from military to civilian leadership in Afghanistan and Iraq.

The Strategic Studies Institute joins the co-editors of this volume in thanking the Bush School staff members for their extraordinary efforts in coordinating the conference and in the preparation of this book. We especially thank the Bush School events coordinator, Beth Stanley. Bush School graduate assistant Ethan Bennett contributed to making the colloquium a success and in laying the groundwork for this volume. The Bush School and SSI also thank Robert Fiedler of the Reserve Officers Association for his outstanding support in hosting the colloquium in the ROA Minuteman Memorial Building in Washington, DC.

The Bush School of Government and Public Service at Texas A&M University is dedicated to academic integrity, leadership development, professional experience, and unique relationships between professors and students academically and in research. The Bush School program also offers students opportunities through national and international internships and emphasizes the development of written and oral communication skills. The Bush School, along with SSI, are proud to put forward this book, as both institutes believe the individual research, analysis, and opinions expressed within are valuable and important to the ongoing debates over national security reform.

DOUGLAS C. LOVELACE, JR.
Director
Strategic Studies Institute

PREFACE

Assessing U.S. leadership in ongoing national security reform was the focus of a research colloquium hosted by the Bush School of Government and Public Service, Texas A&M University; and the Strategic Studies Institute (SSI), U.S. Army War College, on April 22, 2010, in Washington DC. The colloquium was entitled "2010: Preparing for a Mid-Term Assessment of Leadership and National Security Reform in the Obama Administration." The colloquium's three panels addressed: (1) Assessing National Security Reform; (2) Legislative Imperatives; and (3) The Way Forward.

This colloquium and report continue our ongoing partnership with the Strategic Studies Institute and other foreign and defense policy educational and research institutes. There is an important need to think more deeply about leadership and government reform in their broadest sense. This volume includes papers that reassess our theories, concepts, and practices for understanding America's leadership role in national security and international affairs. The following chapters offer a variety of ideas, approaches, and suggestions. While these represent a wide and contrasting range of views, there is a consensus that reforms are needed across and within the many government agencies engaged in diplomacy, defense, and development policy.

Present as panelists and participants were more than two dozen analysts, scholars, and former officials from the executive and legislative branches of government. The majority of the concerns, questions, and ideas discussed during the symposium are articulated and expanded upon in the following chapters. The colloquium co-sponsors included the Reserve Officers Association (ROA), the Foreign Policy Research Institute (FPRI), the Hudson Institute, the Council on Foreign Relations (CFR), the American Security Project (ASP), Creative Associates International, Inc. (CAII), and the Project on National Security Reform (PNSR). The colloquium participants, including experts from both the policy community and academia, all contributed their ideas to address the pressing issues captured in the body of this book. We thank these prestigious research institutions for their participation in this project.

We especially thank the Director of the Strategic Studies Institute, Professor Douglas Lovelace, for co-sponsoring the colloquium, and also SSI's Dr. Robert H. (Robin) Dorff for his efforts in conference planning and execution, as well as for chairing a panel and co-editing this volume. We greatly appreciate the editorial skills of Dr. James Pierce and Ms. Rita Rummel of the Strategic Studies Institute, for their professional and selfless efforts in publishing this monograph. Robert Fiedler of the ROA provided essential support in hosting the colloquium at the ROA Minuteman Memorial Building in Washington, DC.

In addition, our Bush School staff performed numerous tasks in planning and executing the conference. Special thanks to our events coordinator, Beth Stanley, for her professionalism in arranging all our support efforts. Our Bush School Graduate Assistants for Research, Ethan Bennett and Matthew Harber, provided administrative and research assistance as well as their ideas and writing talents in planning for the conference as well as in preparing the papers presented in this volume.

Our mid-term assessment is designed to contribute in a positive manner to the ongoing initiatives for institutional and organizational national security reforms. At the same time, we fully realize that much work remains to be done to improve U.S. and coalition efforts to sustain the essential leadership role of the United States in national security and international affairs. The Bush School is proud to join with SSI to publish this book as a tribute to the ideals of two institutions that strongly believe that the individual research and ideas expressed in the pursuit of public service and the national interest are always valuable and important.

RYAN C. CROCKER
Dean and Executive Professor
Holder of the Edward & Howard
Kruse Endowed Chair
George Bush School of Government
& Public Service
Texas A&M University

CHAPTER 1

INTRODUCTION:
STRATEGIC ASSESSMENTS
AND NATIONAL SECURITY REFORM

Joseph R. Cerami
Jared E. Bennett
Robert H. Dorff

One of the fundamental skills of critical thinking is the ability to assess one's own reasoning. To be good at assessment requires that we consistently take apart our thinking and examine the parts (or elements) for quality.[1]

BACKGROUND

On April 22, 2010, the Reserve Officers Association (ROA), the Foreign Policy Research Institute (FPRI), the Hudson Institute, the Council on Foreign Relations (CFR), the American Security Project (ASP), Creative Associates International, Inc. (CAII), and the Project on National Security Reform (PNSR) participated with the Bush School of Government and Public Service, and the Strategic Studies Institute, U.S. Army War College, in co-sponsoring a colloquium in Washington, DC, on a mid-term assessment of leadership and national security reform in the Obama administration. Three panels discussed "Assessing National Security Reform," "Legislative Imperatives," and "Assessing National Security Reform—The Way Forward." The colloquium theme focused on the need for advancing the research and study of key national security issues, engaging the invited participants in sharing their expertise, and informing interested community members of ways to develop a deeper awareness and understanding of security reform issues facing the U.S. Government by examining the topics of leadership and national security reform.

PANEL 1: ASSESSING NATIONAL SECURITY REFORM

The first panel clarified conceptual questions by outlining the current themes inherent in the national security reform debate. In introducing the panel, Joseph Cerami of the Bush School commented that the panel's first objective was to outline and assess changing national security efforts as they have evolved and adapted during the first 2 years of the Obama administration. The second panel's objective was to detail specific political and organizational challenges in which progress was made during the first 2 years, as well as those obstacles that continue to impede significant and efficient reforms.

The panelists introduced the current terminology and trends, and set the conditions for the colloquium discussions. Integral to this panel was an analysis of how security paradigms and the continuing need for reform might affect the organization, operations, policies, and strategies of the U.S. military in the short term.

Joseph Collins of the National Defense University spoke on Afghanistan. In his examination, Collins made five major points: Two presidents have declared that the War in Afghanistan is of vital importance to the nation; the costs of the war have been high in blood and treasure; the Taliban is weakening, thanks to President Barack Obama's surge; the Karzai government is weak, corrupt, and ineffective; and the

Afghan people are tired of war, coalition forces, and their own government. Collins further questioned the future of the war's success, given the current stress on the Department of Defense (DoD) budget (currently projected to be more than $700 billion/year).

Scott Feil of the Institute for Defense Analyses addressed how assessments are generated within the DoD. Feil examined two categories of assessments, Strategic Assessments and Operational Resource Assessments, subsequently detailing how such assessments contribute to national security solutions. Using as examples the DoD response to the improvised explosive device (IED) and the resurgence of the Army post-Vietnam, Feil concluded that the obstacle encountered in problem solving in government is that it does not focus on the "problem as a whole." Rather, each segment of government proposes solution sets that optimize its own capabilities and interests. He concluded that the government should confront national security as a whole with a focus on optimizing the overall function, which necessarily suboptimizes the individual subordinate processes and organizations.

Thomas Mahnken of Johns Hopkins University and the Naval War College examined U.S. Defense policy and its implications for national security reform. Focusing on the proper division of labor in the government, Mahnken suggested that entities within government abide by their clearly defined roles, recommending that the DoD be used to fight and win wars, and the State Department (DoS) and the U.S. Agency for International Development (USAID) be empowered to support a "whole of government" approach to national security issues.

Harvey Sicherman of FPRI reviewed the best and worst cases of past Presidents' actions in making national security policy, distinguishing between the Harry Truman (White House-State Department partnership) and Richard Nixon (White House dominant) models. He praised the Bush-Baker-Scowcroft (Presidential-led, integrated, interagency process) variant. Sicherman concluded that the current administration has tried a version of the Bush-Baker-Scowcroft model, but too much is being done in the White House. Instead, Sicherman recommended giving greater responsibility to the State Department, allowing the National Security Council (NSC) to focus on its primary mission of coordinating policy for the President while considering policy alternatives.

PANEL 2: THE LEGISLATIVE IMPERATIVE

The second panel, discussing the Legislative Imperative, examined the congressional role in the national security process from 2008 to 2010. Panel Chair James Locher III of the Project on National Security Reform opened the panel by stating that 95 percent of the American people say that national security reform will never be done. Locher went on to refute this point, claiming that the objects impeding reform were: a lack of routine oversight, a lack of confidence, a slow confirmation process for presidential appointees, a failure to pass legislation that has become endemic, and frequent confrontation between the branches of the government. Locher exclaimed that many believe Congress lacks the political will to take on national security reform, but was quick to point out that, quite to the contrary, Goldwater-Nichols achieved just this feat. To elucidate the issue's complexity, Locher identified clear differences between the past and today, with today's challenges being: a security environment that is much more complex, the unprecedented size of the defense budget, and concerns over domestic security. According to Locher, the major challenges confronting national security reform are those of politics, scope, ownership, and bandwidth. Politically, individuals favor the status quo. With regard to scope, Locher emphasized that the size of national security reform is daunting and inhibits congressional commitment. In reference to ownership, Locher stated that the simple fact is that there is no mandate for national security reform. Finally, he stated that bandwidth, or time, is a major challenge, as it took Goldwater-Nichols over 4 years to complete. The focus needed for national security reform would certainly require politicians to surrender other legislative initiatives.

The post-September 11, 2001, system and campaigns in Iraq and Afghanistan have placed additional pressure on the U.S. Government's civilian and military departments and their levels of interagency cooperation. At the heart of this discussion was an assessment of the contributions of the Project on National Security Reform, an initiative on Capitol Hill to build political support for congressional reform of interagency dynamics much in the same way the Goldwater/Nichols Act transformed the armed services.

Nina Serafino of the Congressional Research Service focused on the possibility of legislative action on reform, including reorganizing Congress for proper oversight. Recognizing prospects for comprehensive reform is a daunting task; however, Serafino stated that some members are discussing selected reforms. One example is a national security professional development program to foster interagency cooperation through a civilian interagency education and training program, including rotations between agencies. She noted expert opinion that recommends that Congress reorganize itself cyclically, with small changes made in response to events, and large, substantive changes following periods of rising frustration or party turnover. She reflected that the Obama administration might trigger changes in Congress by submitting a unified security budget combining all security assistance accounts.

Larry Sampler of CAII spoke on the topic of legislative imperatives for national security reform. Sampler said that one of the major impediments to national security reform is the prerogative of an official to seek reelection, thus making things inefficient. The U.S. Government's system of checks and balances creates an environment of stasis, leading to operational paralysis in the government. Sampler also addressed the issue of the terminology being used between military and civilian entities, and the need to understand this terminology to produce effectiveness. Sampler cited the need for good leadership behind national security reform. Finally, Sampler expressed his belief that the 3-Ds (defense, diplomacy, and development) model is not a model based in reality, and should be done away with.

Richard Weitz of the Hudson Institute and PNSR discussed the importance of resource allocation and national security reform. He recommended that the NSC play a greater role in designing an integrated national security process, including new approaches for matching resources to strategies. Weitz also suggested the need for a national operational framework, whereby national security reform would be viewed as more of a national responsibility.

James Lindsay of CFR examined the practicality of national security reform. Specifically, Lindsay tried to answer the questions of why Americans wish to produce reform, and why the government has failed to achieve it. Lindsay suggested that reform is undertaken to elicit greater policy effectiveness. The U.S. Government has failed to achieve reform because of bad policy choices and a streamlined executive. Lindsay also focused on the role of development and its organization within the government, emphasizing the political battles that impede reform. He concluded that reform would be achieved only if the government focused on pivotal reform measures, admitting that the overall political climate would be the eventual catalyst for change.

PANEL 3: ASSESSING NATIONAL SECURITY REFORM – THE WAY FORWARD

This panel focused on examining steps to implement significant national security reform over the next 2 years (2010-12). Panel Chair Robert "Robin" Dorff of the Strategic Studies Institute asked the panelists to assess the Obama administration's first years with an eye toward offering ideas for continuing or accelerating the pace of national security reform. The researchers were also asked to assess the successes and weaknesses of the first years and address the institutional and organizational challenges that continue to face the administration. Finally, the panelists were asked to suggest promising areas for national security reform initiatives in the near term.

Patrick Cronin of the Center for a New American Security stated that one issue confronting the Obama administration is that it has recognized its limits of engagement, especially given the complexity of issues like Iran and North Korea. Cronin criticized the nearsightedness of America by calling for a national security strategy that focused on the future, "thinking about the America of 2030, and not just 2010." Cronin recommended that the United States should focus on civilian capacities and a stronger State Department by developing a better system of educating diplomats, and by recruiting the best and brightest. Cronin also recommended that the United States should become serious about investing in development, focusing on those countries in the bottom realm of the development process, the poorest performers.

Bernard Finel of ASP suggested strengthening the role of the Chairman of the Joint Chiefs of Staff and removing any politics associated with the position. He suggested that this could be achieved by assigning a timeline to the position, such as 5 years without the possibility of removal. In that same vein, he recommended taking the media out of the military, allowing the DoD voice to be expressed through a single office, the Secretary of Defense. Fiscal responsibility was another topic of interest, as Finel stated that declaring wars (those planned for 10, 15, or more years) should be something that is placed on a normal budgeting process. Finel also discussed the legality of behavior in combat by suggesting that there should be an increase in personal liability for criminal conduct.

James Stephenson of CAII examined the areas of counterinsurgency, reconstruction, and stabilization. A focus of the talk was the shrinking role of USAID. Stephenson said it was a great concern that USAID was being taken over by the DoS, further hindering USAID's ability to control its own policy, planning, and budget. The majority of Stephenson's time was spent discussing the role of stabilization and reconstruction. Stephenson said that the individuals who work effectively in stabilization know their territory and can enable the local populace. Stephenson questioned the fiscal sustainability of the current DoS-led civilian efforts in Afghanistan and Pakistan, which use large numbers of U.S. temporary hires who are expensive and lack the training, the experience, or the mobility to be effective.

Beth Tritter of The Glover Park Group explored the debate over development, questioning where it fits in the approach to national security. Tritter agreed that the 3-D's approach is an incorrect model and further addressed the question of whether or not development was truly essential to U.S. foreign policy. Tritter suggested that Secretary of Defense Robert Gates was making development an issue because it takes work off of the hands of the DoD. Tritter also commented on deficits and current spending levels, saying that this will be the catalyst for reform.

KEYNOTE SPEAKER: JAMES CARAFANO, HERITAGE FOUNDATION

The Keynote Speaker, James Carafano, tackled national security reform with regard to defense spending and congressional oversight effectiveness. First, Carafano addressed the overarching sentiment of pessimism in America today, the belief in the idea that we cannot afford defense measures. Carafano defended the position that defense is the fundamental responsibility of the government. He further stated that the proposition for cutting defense spending often becomes an excuse for inaction. Carafano also spoke on the topic of Congress, suggesting that it is incapable of doing functional assessments of national security. He said this is because of the fact that the majority of power is being held by the Senate and House leadership, not in the committees. This produces committee hearings that are almost irrelevant, allowing little time to be given to pertinent, substantial issues. He also directly addressed whole-of-government reform, coupling it with the recommendation that there is a need to define this concept more clearly. Carafano concluded by stating that the government should build an effective construct for the whole of government, and the nation's leadership needs to build a conceptual doctrine in strategic, operational, and tactical terms. According to Carafano, this will allow the government to focus more directly on national security issues that are nonlinear and highly complex.

CONCLUDING THOUGHTS

While there was no consensus among the panelists, three major themes did emerge from the presentations and discussions. First, the initiatives for the extensive national security reform that are required to meet current threats will have to come from outside of the executive branch bureaucracy. This is true, even though former senior members of the Project on National Security Reform hold key executive branch positions.

A second major point was that the 3-Ds model has been a harmful way to portray the capacities, requirements, and relationships for policy and operational effectiveness, especially in ongoing counterinsurgency operations in Afghanistan. In the view of several stability and reconstruction expert field hands with extensive on-the-ground experience, the current 3-Ds model is incorrect, since these functions are not properly represented by circles, are not the same size in terms of capacity and resources and, in many significant ways, do not overlap in several respects in the key areas necessary for effective integration, alignment, and coordination.

Third, the Obama administration still has much work to do in organizing development efforts to focus on the need for stronger political, economic, and social development structures, resources, and leadership. Given the ongoing efforts in Iraq and Afghanistan, there is an urgent need for better definition of the roles and responsibilities of the DoS, the DoD, and USAID.

The following papers and authors' insights in assessing early strategy and reform efforts reflect on the need for improving strategies, as well as the need for more effective assessments. Regarding the need for improving congressional oversight, James Carafano argues for improving our assessment of the whole-of-government construct and the interagency process, as well as for designing fiscally responsible methods for linking policy, operations, and practice. Bernard Finel critically assesses the current state of U.S. civil-military relations and the deficiencies in strategic, cost-benefit analyses. James Locher, the guiding force in the national security reform movement, assesses congressional roles and responsibilities. In assessing national security reform efforts, Richard Weitz sees a need for more comprehensive national security reviews that address capabilities, needs, and resources, as well as for improving our strategic knowledge management. FPRI's Harvey Sicherman provides historical and current insights on the presidency and Cabinet versus NSC tensions and the need for attention in terms of both policymaking structures and functions.

Reforming U.S. national security policymaking, especially policy implementation, remains a work in progress among and within government, nongovernment, and private organizations. The purpose of this book is to reflect on the idea that the national security community should place renewed attention on, and more-critical thinking about, improving strategic assessment processes as well.

ENDNOTES - CHAPTER 1

1. Richard Paul and Linda Elder, *Critical Thinking: Learn the Tools the Best Thinkers Use,* Upper Saddle River, NJ: Pearson, Prentice Hall, 2006, p. 43.

CHAPTER 2

GRADING THE GOVERNMENT: A MID-TERM NATIONAL SECURITY ASSESSMENT

James Jay Carafano

INTRODUCTION

The way America manages and maintains the key instruments of national security has slipped into neutral. Frankly, there are few signs that the trend is likely to change any time soon. Two of the biggest obstacles to making progress are: (1) an increasingly Washington-wide belief that that the United States cannot afford to defend itself; and (2) an equally dour belief that mastering interagency and whole-of-government operations are just too difficult, or that mastering them requires the impossible task of completely reconfiguring how Washington works. Both these beliefs are wrong-headed, and if they don't change, America will slip from neutral into reverse.

The issue of defense spending is both highly controversial and political. There is an overreaching pessimism that the United States cannot afford defense measures. One of the best examples of this is the debate on the ballistic missile defense program. Spending on this important project does not even account for 1 percent of the defense budget in Fiscal Year (FY) 2011, and is $1 billion less than the Bush administration's budget request for missile defense in FY 2009.[1] Such cuts are trumpeted as cost-saving measures and proof that Washington is capable of making hard choices; in fact, the exact opposite is true. The mantra of cutting

13

defense as a strategic priority in order to address the nation's fiscal ills has become a convenient excuse to justify politically expedient decisions.

Whole-of-government reform has become an equally convoluted Gordian knot.[2] Everyone acknowledges that the most pressing national security challenges require the effective integration of multiple federal agencies. Likewise, there is a consensus that the U.S. Government often fails to muster effective joint action in times of crisis or great need. Most, however, also believe that fixing this shortfall is just too hard or requires restructuring the federal bureaucracy from top to bottom. Painting the problem as a difficulty akin to the labors of Hercules encourages most in Washington to adopt the politically convenient answer: do nothing.

WASHINGTON'S PHONY WAR—THE GUNS AND BUTTER BATTLE

The U.S. defense budget has suffered from a dangerous, post-Cold War trend: It has been slowly eroding, interspersed with event-driven massive increases to pay for current operations. This yin and yang of spending has undermined the development of a stable, coherent defense program.[3] Today, national defense ranks a distant fourth in the overall budget, trailing financial support for the elderly (through Social Security and Medicare), education funding, and means-tested welfare payments. In terms of national spending, defense is actually at near historic lows. All defense spending (military operations in Afghanistan and Iraq included) is equal to about half of what the United States spent on average each year (as a percentage of gross domestic product [GDP]) throughout the Cold War.[4]

Defense spending is less than one-fifth of the federal budget. Nevertheless, it was the target of roughly half of the administration's $17 billion in spending cuts in 2010.[5] As many as 50 programs were cut or eliminated in the past year alone,[6] nor is there an end to the cutting of the defense budget in sight. The Obama administration has proposed cutting the C-17 Transport Plane ($2.5 billion); EP-X Manned Airborne Intelligence, Surveillance, Reconnaissance and Targeting Aircraft ($12 million), or the Navy's CGX Cruiser Program, known also as Next Generation Cruiser Program ($46 million).[7]

Entitlement spending and the sum of all other discretionary spending account for most of the federal budget. Federal, state, and local governments consume over 40 percent of U.S. GDP.[8] Given that proportion, even large cuts in the defense budget would not reign in federal spending or reduce the federal deficit. In the not-so-distant past, Congress has eagerly showered checks for hundreds of billions of dollars on dicey financial gambits like the Troubled Asset Relief Program (TARP) or the demonstrably nonstimulating "stimulus package."[9] Legislation such as health care and cap and trade (the latter has to be passed in the Senate yet) will add multi-trillion-dollar expenses, even further straining the budget.

Taking all of the above into account, military spending (including the costs of all the battles in the global war on terrorism) looks pretty modest. Certainly, defense, despite the heated rhetoric from Washington, is not the source of the nation's fiscal ills. The way America is going, the federal debt will be $4.8 trillion in just 5 years. By then, the interest payment on the debt alone will exceed the entire defense budget.

Lack of funding will inevitably lead to a lack in capabilities. The military has missions that cannot be compromised without putting the United States at risk. It has to protect the homeland and respond to domestic disasters, ensure freedom of the commons (air, space, sea, and cyberspace) for commerce; help build the capacity of other allies to defend themselves and partner with the United States to defend common interests; and have the capability to breach the sanctuary of the nation's enemies — conventional and nonconventional, state or nonstate — so that they have no home base from which they can attack the United States with impunity. All these missions are performed today, but the military strains to do so with the forces available. The notion that long-term national defense can be provided for with significantly fewer forces and capabilities defies common sense.

The government has put off modernizing many major systems (such as ground vehicles) for decades. Procurement holidays are unprecedented since the Great Depression, and unparalleled for a nation at war. To make matters worse, the United States never recapitalized its forces after the Cold War. Thus, calls for another peace-dividend now are the equivalent of taking a peace-dividend on the back of what in many ways is still a peacetime force.

It is necessary to maintain current levels of defense spending and implement comprehensive reforms to prevent a debilitating investment crisis in defense. For example, the average age of the Air Force inventory is 23 years, and there are no plans to replace it.[10] According to Air Force estimates, 800 aircraft will be lacking by 2024, and Navy officials projected a shortfall of up to 200 aircraft by 2018.[11]

The broad range of missions performed today requires steady, robust funding for several years. In addition, the services will need billions of dollars for at least 3 years after operations in Iraq conclude to repair and replace equipment damaged during combat operations.[12] For years the Department of Defense (DoD) has not addressed the issue of shortfalls (differences between service requirements and money allocated to fulfill these requirements in the budget) because of the dynamic of wars and budget supplementals.[13]

Predictable levels of defense spending would allow the military to reset, rebuild, and modernize arsenals and train forces for all types of warfare. However, forcing the military to make unnecessary trade-offs, accepting too much risk, assuming that the potential threats will never materialize, or not reducing global military commitments in line with changes in defense strategy could ultimately produce a hollow force that is unready, unable, or too small to help keep the nation safe, free, and prosperous.

Soft power, the use of diplomacy, and other tools of national security are not necessarily fungible. Soft power is not a substitute for hard power. Indeed, soft power is at its most effective when it is used in concert with hard power. Gutting defense will not only do little to revitalize the U.S. economy; it will unbalance and undermine all the nation's instruments of national power.

WASHINGTON'S FAINT OF HEART ON WHOLE-OF-GOVERNMENT

In addition to losing its will to fund national defense, Washington has become positively inert on addressing the challenges of harnessing all the instru-

17

ments of national power on tough issues. Here, much of the fault lies with Congress, as well as with the administration that has not pressed Congress to do the right thing.

The poster child for the lack of integrated effort is the challenge of homeland security. There is no question that Congress has a major role to play in establishing an effective homeland security regime. While the Homeland Security Act of 2002 created a lead federal agency for many domestic security activities, this was only the first step. Building an effective Department of Homeland Security (DHS) requires sound strategies, solid programs, personnel reforms, and integrating information technologies; effective congressional oversight is a key part of making these initiatives happen.[14] Congress, however, has failed to provide competent leadership.

The final report of the September 11, 2001 (9/11) Commission reaffirmed the importance of fixing congressional oversight. The commission held that:

> Congress should create a single, principal point of oversight and review for homeland security. Congressional leaders are best able to judge what committee should have jurisdiction over this department [the DHS] and its duties. But we believe Congress has the obligation to choose one in the House and one in the Senate, and that this committee should be a permanent standing committee with a nonpartisan staff.[15]

One expert witness appearing before the commission testified that the lack of effective congressional oversight is perhaps the single greatest obstacle impeding the successful development of the DHS.[16]

Today, there are at least 100 committees, subcommittees, and other entities claiming jurisdiction over the DHS. Congressional oversight is both proper and necessary, but the high number of hearings decreases their relevance and provides little time for pertinent substantial issues—in addition to creating burdensome duplications, consuming resources, and devouring the time of the DHS staff.

Fixing this conundrum of oversight would require collapsing jurisdiction into single committees with responsibility for homeland security oversight in the House and Senate—such a reform ought to be a priority. Yet neither the leadership in the Congress nor the White House has shown any serious interest in taking such a step.

BIGGER-THAN-A-BREADBOX PROBLEMS

Beyond homeland security, many federal missions require better integration, the foundation of which is whole-of-government reform. The manner of U.S. interagency operations has changed little since the end of the Cold War. Innovations are needed to create a regional framework for interagency planning and action. To understand the performance of the interagency process, it is useful to divide it into three levels: policy, operations, and practice. At the policy level, agencies in Washington reach broad agreement on what each will do to coordinate and support an overall U.S. policy. At the lowest level is the practice of cooperation among individuals on the ground.[17]

It is at the operational level where the U.S. Government undertakes major operations and campaigns and where agencies in Washington have to develop operational plans such as coordinating recovery operations after a major hurricane. This is where interagency cooperation is the weakest, a legacy of the

Cold War. There was never a requirement for federal agencies to do that kind of integrated planning to contain the Soviet Union. Agencies generally agreed on the broad role each would play. There were few requirements under which they had to plan to work together in the field to accomplish a goal under unified direction. Washington has never had an enduring formal system to do that.

The United States needs to improve its ability to coordinate major interagency challenges outside of Washington, away from the offices of Cabinet secretaries and staffs, whether it is coordinating disaster relief over a three-state area after a hurricane, or conducting the occupation of a foreign country. In short, the challenge here lies not in the formulation of national policy, but in planning and executing operations in a way that lets the people on the ground work well together and get the job done. Especially at the federal level, centralization and dissolution of responsibilities of federal agencies complicates the process of governing, obfuscates effective congressional oversight, blurs lines of authority and responsibility, and increasingly bogs the White House down in the day-to-day affairs of managing homeland security.[18]

There are many reasons interagency cooperation is weakest at the operational level. Flaws come from: the traditional divide between civil and military spheres; distinct institutional cultures and operational organization; lack of common knowledge, practices, and experiences that would facilitate trust and confidence among participants at the interagency process; and lack of capabilities to conduct operational activities. In addition, federal inspector general corps responsible for oversight, efficiency, and credibility align with individual agencies instead of providing common ground for interagency operations. Ultimately, the question is: What can be done to make the interagency process more responsive in the operational environment?

One major shortfall in the interagency process is the lack of adequate capacity to conduct operations outside of Washington. Where the lead agency has the preponderance of responsibility and resources, other departments usually act like bystanders, primarily interested in doing as little as possible. There is little cooperation or planning with outside organizations or departments.

Congress is ill-suited to promote cooperation between federal agencies. It appropriates funds for operations of individual departments and the jurisdiction of committees that oversee the government dovetail with the departments they oversee. Also, many politicians are rightly uncomfortable with the notion of big government. They are concerned that creating a more effective interagency process would empower government to the point that it might lead to abuse, encouraging Washington to take on missions that are not appropriate.

While Congress has done much to promote interagency inertia, the administration has done little to break the log jam. Nothing will change unless Washington starts doing something different.

How can we break out of this morass and start making real progress toward preparing effectively for the worst? The Constitution suggests an answer. The framers were most interested in articulating the roles, responsibilities, and checks and balances between the branches of government. They left it to responsible men and women within each branch to largely determine how to run their part of the government. Thus, the answer is: We need each part of government to do its job, and we need responsible people.

Real reform has to start with Congress. It must set a legislative framework that ensures the Executive branch can stock federal agencies with responsible people who are skilled in interagency operations. Each chamber should establish a new committee with very narrow jurisdiction to address only those matters that are essential to building a federal work force skilled at whole-of-government operations. The committees should have oversight for the policies establishing the education, assignment, and accreditation of interagency leaders in the federal enterprise. Such committees could provide the needed, but currently still lacking, leadership.

GETTING BACK ON TRACK

Unless Washington takes two critical steps—adequately funding national defense and fixing congressional oversight of interagency operations—the instruments of national security are likely to get rustier in the years ahead.

ENDNOTES - CHAPTER 2

1. Baker Spring, "The Obama Administration's Ballistic Missile Defense Program: Treading Water in Shark-Infested Seas," Heritage Foundation *Backgrounder* No. 2396, April 8, 2010, available from *http://www.heritage.org/Research/Reports/2010/04/The-Obama-Administrations-Ballistic-Missile-Defense-Program-Treading-Water-in-Shark-Infested-Seas*.

2. Whole-of-government reform is an approach encompassing interagency operations; coordinating the joint effort of multiple government agencies, often with support from the ministries from different nations and nongovernmental and international organizations; as well as private sector service providers (entities that often have different operational styles and practices, con-

trasting organizational cultures, disparate resources, and conflicting goals and missions).

3. Kevin N. Lewis, "The Discipline Gap and Other Reasons for Humility and Realism in Defense Planning," in Paul K. Davis, ed., *New Challenges for Defense Planning: Rethinking How Much Is Enough,* Santa Monica, CA: RAND Corporation, 1994, p. 104.

4. Jim Talent, "A Constitutional Basis for Defense," Heritage Foundation *America at Risk Memo* No. AR 10-006, June 1, 2010, available from *www.heritage.org/research/reports/2010/06/A-Constitutional-Basis-for-Defense.*

5. Baker Spring, "The 2011 Defense Budget: Inadequate and Full of Inconsistencies," Heritage Foundation *Backgrounder* No. 2375, February 22, 2010, available from *thf_media.s3.amazonaws.com/2010/pdf/bg2375.pdf.*

6. John T. Bennett, "DoD Examining F/A-18 Multiyear Plans; Gates Endorses KC-X Requirements," *Defense News,* March 24, 2010, available from *www.defensenews.com/story.php?i=4553123.*

7. Ed O'Keefe, "2011 Budget: Spending Cuts and Reductions," *The Washington Post,* February 1, 2010, available from *voices.washingtonpost.com/federal-eye/2010/02/2011_budget_spending_cuts_and.html.*

8. Organisation for Economic Co-operation and Development, *Economic Outlook 86 Database,* available from *www.oecd.org/dataoecd/5/51/2483816.xls.*

9. James Carafano, "War Spending Is Not Frivolous Spending," Heritage Foundation *Commentary,* December 1, 2009, available from *www.heritage.org/Research/Commentary/2009/12/War-Spending-is-Not-Frivolous-Spending.*

10. Talent.

11. Ronald O'Rourke, "Navy-Marine Corps Strike-Fighter Shortfall: Background and Options for Congress," *Report for Congress,* Washington, DC: Congressional Research Service, May 12, 2008, p. 4, available from *www.fas.org/sgp/crs/weapons/RS22875.pdf.*

12. Mackenzie Eaglen, "U.S. Defense Spending: The Mismatch Between Plans and Resources," Heritage Foundation *Backgrounder* No. 2418, p. 3, available from *www.heritage.org/research/reports/2010/06/us-defense-spending-the-mismatch-between-plans-and-resources#_ftnl*.

13. David Berteau, "Fixing the Shortfalls: Defense Budget Trends and Long Term Impact," *Defense Industrial Initiatives Group Current Issues*, Washington, DC: Center for Strategic and International Studies, No. 19, December 14, 2009, p. 1, available from *csis.org/files/publication/DIIG%20Current%20Issue%20Number%2019%20Fixing%20the%20Shortfalls%20Defense%20Budget%20Trends%20and%20Long%20Term%20Impact%20_0.pdf*.

14. James Carafano, "Homeland Security Needs Responsible Congressional Oversight," Heritage Foundation *WebMemo* No. 528, July 7, 2004, available from *www.heritage.org/Research/Reports/2004/07/Homeland-Security-Needs-Responsible-Congressional-Oversight*.

15. *The 9/11 Commission Report: National Commission on Terrorist Attacks Upon the United States*, p. 421, available from *www.gpoaccess.gov/911/pdf/fullreport.pdf*.

16. James Jay Carafano and David Heyman, "DHS 2.0: Rethinking the Department of Homeland Security," Heritage Foundation *Special Report* No. SR-02, December 13, 2004, available from *www.heritage.org/Research/Reports/2004/12/DHS-20-Rethinking-the-Department-of-Homeland-Security*.

17. James Jay Carafano, "Herding Cats: Understanding Why Government Agencies Don't Cooperate and How to Fix the Problem," Heritage Foundation *Lecture* No. 955, July 26, 2006, available from *www.heritage.org/research/lecture/herding-cats-understanding-why-government-agencies-dont-cooperate-and-how-to-fix-the-problem*.

18. Jena Baker McNeill and James Carafano, "President Should Merge Homeland Security Council with NSC," Heritage Foundation *WebMemo* #2390, April 9, 2009, available from *www.heritage.org/Research/Reports/2009/04/President-Should-Merge-Homeland-Security-Council-with-NSC*.

CHAPTER 3

FIVE HERETICAL SUGGESTIONS: ADDRESSING CIVIL-MILITARY TENSIONS

Bernard I. Finel

INTRODUCTION

Over the past several years, Washington, DC, has been consumed with another in a periodic round of hand-wringing over the structure of the national security process. The main thrust of these efforts has been an attempt to deal with supposed gaps in America's capacity to coordinate whole-of-government responses, particularly in counterinsurgency situations as in Iraq and Afghanistan. The recommendations have usually focused on better integration of the various instruments of statecraft, as well as better training and education for civilians to produce a unified cohort of national security professionals. This entire line of argumentation is both flawed and misguided.

At a fundamental level, much of the debate over national security reform has been distorted by the unexamined assumption that it is in America's interest to maintain a quasi-colonial presence abroad. Efforts to implement reforms in support of that objective run into the problem that this approach simply does not support American national security, and the tensions between any objective assessment of the challenges facing the United States and the supposed demands of this imperial mission create an endless series of unsolvable problems. On the other hand, over the past decade, there have been three sets of crises in the national security process. Identifying the problems with greater clarity allows for a more consistent and sustainable path forward.

First, there is indeed a problem surrounding the occupation/counterinsurgency/counterterrorism (CT)/hybrid war nexus, but the problem is not the lack of a capacity to wage such conflicts using a whole-of-government approach. The problem is in the failure to impose a disciplined cost-benefit analysis framework to the issue, and the associated failure to develop an explicit risk-management framework for these sorts of conflicts. These conflicts involve actual costs and opportunity costs, few of which have been explicitly assessed against likely benefits from the endeavors.

Second, there is an ongoing crisis in civil-military relations. The consequence of unhealthy civil-military relations has resulted in a paradoxical rise of military entrepreneurs freelancing on policy issues, combined with a failure to systematically integrate professional military advice into policy decisions. Though these two problems seem contradictory at first glance, they actually represent two sides of the same coin. They both result from a breakdown in a disciplined and principled scheme for civil-military relations. We need a system in which responsible military advise can be delivered to senior decisionmakers, while at the same time discouraging what has become a back-channel-policy development process whereby military leaders curry opinion leaders in think tanks and the press directly.[1]

Third, the United States national security community has, over the past decade, been implicated in an egregious series of unlawful activities. These have included battlefield war crimes and their cover-up, unlawful domestic surveillance, torture and other inhumane treatment of prisoners, and a wide variety of criminal acts committed by individuals on U.S. Government contracts.[2] These acts are a tremendous embarrassment and pose a threat both to American foreign policy and domestic liberty. The national security community needs to operate within the confines of domestic and international law. It is doing neither in too many cases.

In order to address the three sets of challenges, I propose five heretical recommendations. None of these have been discussed in the national security reform debates in any depth, but they have the advantage of: (a) dealing with some pressing crises in the national security community, and (b) that they can be accomplished without spending billions or re-engineering vast segments of the U.S. government.

THE ROLE OF THE CHAIRMAN OF THE JOINT CHIEFS

The Chairman of the Joint Chiefs of Staff (CJCS) ought to be better insulated from political pressures. The CJCS needs to be able to provide candid advice to the President and Congress about military issues. If that is to be the case, he needs to be above political pressures. He is not in the chain of command in any case, so there is no issue of civilian control involved in insulating him. However, there are real negative consequences to the Chief being muzzled by directives that "the Department of Defense [DoD] speaks with one voice," or the pressure associated with the implicit threat of being removed for being at odds with administration policy, or not being reappointed to a customary second term as happened with General Peter Pace.

Like the director of the Federal Bureau of Investigation or the Chairman of the Federal Reserve, the CJCS should be appointed for a 5-7 year term, Senate confirmable, but removable only for causes like the abuse of office for personal gain. The CJCS should be charged by statute with providing the President not just with his best advice, but with serving as a conduit for formal dissents from within the military—creating something akin to the State Department's dissent channel.[3]

There would be many benefits to this approach. First, the President would have more reliable access to independent, professional military advice. Second, various CJCS products, including the Chairman's Risk Assessment, would be more candid and honest. Third, this approach would create a channel for military dissent and hopefully reduce the amount of back-channel lobbying and diminish the opportunities for military policy entrepreneurs.

Consider recent cases. A strong, independent chairman would have been able to give additional weight to the concerns of Generals Tommy Franks and Eric Shinseki about inadequate forces being budgeted for the initial invasion of Iraq. He could have given voice and standing to the concerns of the Judge Advocate General Corps (JAGC) regarding violations of international law in our treatment of detainees. He could, in 2006 and 2010, been more candid about identifying the flaws and limits in the *Quadrennial Defense Reviews* of those years. In 2009, he could have been more effective in advising President Barack Obama's Afghanistan review that recommended a counterinsurgency approach in Afghanistan without any sense of the resource implications of that decision.[4]

PUBLIC VISIBILITY OF OTHER GENERAL OFFICERS

In contrast to the greater role for the CJCS, it is imperative that other general officers see their profile diminished. In 2009, the United States was treated to the public spectacle of a theater commander publicly debating the Vice-President of the United States on a critical policy issue. This is a shocking level of insubordination, similar to General Douglas MacArthur's breach of protocol during the Korean War. In 2010, General Stanley McChrystal was ultimately fired for the lack of judgment demonstrated in various quotes given by him and his aides to a *Rolling Stone* reporter.[5]

But General McChrystal was not the first to transgress norms of civil-military relations. Indeed, a large number of political generals over the past several years have routinely been crossing the line into policy advocacy. For instance, General Michael Hayden, as the Central Intelligence Agency (CIA) Director, was a key architect of an unlawful domestic surveillance program and proceeded to provide many of the public rationales. General David Petraeus, of course, was the face of the Iraq surge in 2007, but he also issued pronouncements on the Arab-Israeli dispute, and in August 2010 launched a media blitz to weaken President Obama's announced timeline in Afghanistan.[6] He later issued a press release directly calling out American citizens for exercising, albeit in a misguided fashion, their First Amendment rights to free speech.[7] Engaging publicly in these policy debates goes beyond the traditional role of military officers in lobbying for service-specific programs. Decisions about war and peace, about the balance between civil liberties and security, and politically complex issues like Middle East peace must remain in the civilian sphere if the concept of civilian primacy is to mean anything.

A fundamental challenge is that in the United States we have come to so venerate military service that the moment a military leader weighs in on an issue supporting him or her, it becomes a test of patriotism. The question ceases to be the strategic issue under consideration and instead becomes about supporting the military. This also serves to politicize the military in ways that are not conducive to sound civil-military relations. When the liberal activist group Move On took out ads challenging "General Betray Us," they cross a line of respectful dialogue, and yet it was a natural consequence of Petraeus willingly taking on the role of administration spokesman for an unpopular war.[8] As a consequence and for the benefit of both civilian supremacy and military professionalism, this sort of involvement in policy debates needs to be restrained.

Serving General officers, other than the CJCS, should be banned from any public statements. They should not give speeches to think tanks or universities, nor give interviews to TV or newspapers. They should communicate only through the chain of command and when responding to direct questions in congressional hearings.

LIMIT GENERALS AS POLITICAL APPOINTEES

Another major cause of the politicization of the military is the now-routine tapping of recently retired officers to serve as political appointees. The ability to reward military officers for following unlawful or other politically sensitive orders with high-prestige appointments risks politicizing the military and erodes professionalism in the officer corps.

As a consequence, no retired general officer should be eligible for any political appointment for a period of no less than 5 years after retirement from the service. Nor should any serving general be eligible to run any government agency (including Department of Defense agencies). This would make a dramatic change in the culture of several DoD agencies, but as a practical matter, an agency head ought to be a civilian because of the position's inherent policymaking role.

The example of Michael Hayden is too serious to ignore. Hayden developed and implemented an unlawful domestic surveillance program; indeed, as initially implemented, it was denied recertification even by the Bush administration. He was then rewarded with a promotion to head the CIA immediately upon his retirement from active duty.

NATIONAL SECURITY EXPENDITURES SHOULD FOLLOW PAYGO UNLESS WAR IS DECLARED

PAYGO is a congressional rule whereby all new expenditures must be offset with either revenue increases or spending cuts making them budget neutral. PAYGO was used to great effect in the 1990s, leading to dramatically reduced budget deficits and actual surpluses from 1998 to 2001. Placing war supplementals off-budget and refusing to even consider spending or revenue off-sets makes waging drawn-out conflicts with few national security benefits too easy politically. The United States should be able to use force in defense of the national interest, but using force should only be done in circumstances where the threat is significant enough to justify additional revenues or spending cuts as part of the price of doing business.

Regardless of whether the United States national security actually benefits from the extended occupations of Iraq and Afghanistan, it is doubtful that these conflicts could be termed cost-effective. Consider the importance of the CT mission in justifying the escalation of the conflict in Afghanistan. Certainly, there are some CT benefits to a greater presence in Afghanistan and a continued suppression of the insurgency, but is the United States really getting $100 billion worth of CT annually from the effort? By placing these conflicts largely outside normal budgeting channels, American leaders have largely ignored the tradeoffs associated with waging long, drawn-out, nation-building campaigns.

CLARIFY PERSONAL LIABILITY FOR CRIMINAL ACTS

In the name of the War on Terror, the United States has essentially accepted what was once a punchline as a national policy, "If the president does it, it isn't illegal." And just as bad, the United States has decided that the Nuremberg Defense, "I was just following orders," is legitimate.[9] It would have been hard enough to overturn the Bush administration's precedents; it will be essentially impossible to overturn bipartisan precedent from both Presidents George Bush and Obama.

As painful as the American experience with independent counsels, particularly Ken Starr's lurid investigation into President Bill Clinton, has been, the experience of the Obama administration has demonstrated the fundamental problem with leaving these sorts of investigations in the hands of future administrations. It is difficult to imagine a president investigating the national security choices of his predecessor. By the same token, however, the current precedent provides no deterrence against unlawful acts committed in the name of national security. This is a fundamental threat to our constitutional order.

While it would be ideal if we could rely on professionalism to restrain unlawful conduct, the reality is that, absent some possibility of criminal liability, the pressure to simply go along is likely to be difficult to refuse. There needs, in short, to be some independent authority capable of investigating and initiating criminal proceedings for actions such as war crimes and unlawful intelligence activities.

CONCLUSIONS

The United States currently faces a number of significant foreign policy challenges, but we will not be able to meet those challenges until and unless we address some of the major problems that have emerged over the past decade. Most notably, the United States has expended billions of dollars in unnecessary and often incompetently waged conflicts in Iraq and Afghanistan, demonstrating that effective military advice is not being well integrated into policymaking decisions.

Worse, the consequence of this decade of war has been a dramatic erosion in civil-military norms to the point that egregious violations of these norms is so commonplace as to pass largely without notice. The great risk is not of a military coup, of course, but rather of a continued politicization of the U.S. military in a way that makes the effective integration of military power into American national security strategy even more difficult.

There is a strong temptation to address problems that will help us win the wars we are in. This drives the admirable desire to develop better whole-of-government approaches to issues like counterinsurgency, but prioritizing this approach assumes that such wars are either inevitable or beneficial. As a practical matter, neither one of those claims is at all self-evident. Addressing some of the major challenges in the provision of military advice, the politicization of the military, and the erosion of civil-military norms of professionalism would serve a dual purpose: It would both ensure that civilian supremacy, a key value in a democracy, is protected, and it would likely provide benefits in the form of more effective security strategy decisionmaking.

Many U.S. problems in Iraq and Afghanistan stemmed from a failure to integrate military advice into key decisions. By doing so better, the United States may not only have a better chance to win the wars we are in, but also to avoid those kind of lingering conflicts whose costs easily outweigh any conceivable strategic benefit.

ENDNOTES - CHAPTER 3

1. This paragraph was written prior to General Stanley McChrystal's problems following the publication of a profile in *Rolling Stone* magazine. That development merely strengthens the assessment of this essay.

2. Jane Mayer, *The Dark Side*, New York: Anchor, 2009 ; Jack Goldsmith, *The Terror Presidency*, New York: W.W. Norton, 2009.

3. *Foreign Affairs Manual Vol. 2, General, Policy 2 FAM 070*, Washington, DC: U.S. Department of State, available from *www.state.gov/documents/organization/84374.pdf*.

4. Rajiv Chandrasekaran, "Civilian, Military Officials at Odds Over Resources Needed for Afghan Counterinsurgency," *Washington Post,* October 8, 2009, available from *www.washingtonpost.com/wp-dyn/content/article/2009/10/07/AR2009100704088.html.*

5. Michael Hastings, "The Runaway General," *Rolling Stone,* June 22, 2010, available from *www.rollingstone.com/politics/news/17390/119236.*

6. Associated Press, "Hayden insists warrantless surveillance is legal," MSNBC, available from *www.msnbc.msn.com/id/12847084/*; Rajiv Chandrasekaran, "Gen. David Petraeus says Afghanistan war strategy 'fundamentally sound'," *Washington Post,* August 16, 2010, available from *www.washingtonpost.com/wp-dyn/content/article/2010/08/15/AR2010081501514.html.*

7. Julian E. Barnes and Matthew Rosenberg, "Petraeus Condemns U.S. Church's Plan to Burn Qurans," *Wall Street Journal,* September 6, 2010.

8. Wikipedia provides a comprehensive review of the controversy that is available from *en.wikipedia.org/wiki/MoveOn.org_ad_controversy.*

9. Daphne Eviatar, "In Torture Cases, Obama Toes Bush Line," *Washington Independent,* "March 16, 2009, available from *washingtonindependent.com/33985/in-torture-cases-obama-toes-bush-line.*

CHAPTER 4

CONGRESSIONAL NATIONAL SECURITY REFORM DURING THE OBAMA ADMINISTRATION

James R. Locher III

INTRODUCTION

As an equal branch of government, Congress plays a crucial role in national security affairs, and Capitol Hill's participation in the reform of the national security system is essential to the ultimate success of this endeavor. With the legislative power to authorize and appropriate resources, Congress can spearhead and direct reform through its oversight of the application, administration, and execution of the laws it passes. While national security reform is a sizeable undertaking, Congress successfully completed the difficult transformation of the Department of Defense (DoD) with the Goldwater-Nichols Act of 1986. Admittedly, today's national security environment has changed considerably from that of the 1980s. Several challenges must be overcome in Congress to ensure success, including issues of institutional knowledge, politics, and capacity. Overcoming these challenges will require reform in the legislative branch itself.

Comprehensive restructuring is critically needed to revamp our out-of-date national security system, which was devised to address the Cold War threats of a bipolar, state-centric world. In the post-World War II environment, stove-piped agencies and departments were responsible for applying the elements of national power with only a marginal need for interagency coordination. The President benefited from the National Security Council, established by the National Security Act of 1947. Its members were drawn from the agencies and departments with purviews relevant to national security. This arrangement, however, has proved ill suited for the current threat environment, which is characterized by tensions among a complex array of state, substate, and transnational entities, and is further complicated by the dynamics of technological advancements and globalization. The new national security threats require a careful calibration of the instruments of national power enabled by robust coordination across the interagency community.

Capitol Hill's organization mirrors that of the executive branch. Individual committees are charged with overseeing specific agencies and departments. However, since Congress does not have a National Security Act of its own to encourage a holistic approach to national security affairs, it remains focused on its parts. Its inability to look at the national security system comprehensively has rendered Congress unable to address whole-of-government integration, which is now the central challenge of the national security system.

Two key deficiencies result from the legislature's stove-piped approach to national security. First, through its excessive focus on the parts, Congress has a tendency to reinforce divisions in the executive branch, magnifying interagency gaps and cleavages. Second, Congress is becoming increasingly irrelevant to the larger issues of national security, as it lacks an institutional mechanism to address issues that cut across agency lines.

One reason for this is the current committee system, which causes two notable dynamics. By depriving any congressional body of the explicit jurisdiction to authorize, fund, or oversee interagency solutions, congressional committees examine issues from the narrow confines of particular agency perspectives. Furthermore, stove-piped programming is reinforced by an appropriations process driven by committee jurisdictions rather than a mission-based budgetary practice that would be more akin to a whole-of-government approach.

The Project on National Security Reform's (PNSR) report, *Forging a New Shield,* identified six major problems in congressional performance in national security affairs. They are as follows:

1. Congress undertakes no routine oversight of interagency issues, operations, or requirements;

2. Congress lacks interest and confidence in the executive branch's management of foreign affairs;

3. The allocation of resources by Congress tends towards inflexibility;

4. Slow confirmation processes for presidential appointees by the Senate lead to inaction and bureaucratic drift on many issues;

5. The failure to pass legislation on time has become endemic;

6. The legislative and executive branches are too confrontational.[1]

Given these problems, there is considerable need for Congress to reform itself in order to further comprehensive national security transformation. Unfortunately, there has been no meaningful action on this front to date.

Even so, Capitol Hill has been acutely interested in reforming the executive branch apparatus in an effort to keep it responsive to changing national security imperatives. Through its oversight role, Congress seeks to promote efficiency, economy, effectiveness, responsiveness, and accountability among the executive agencies and departments. Nevertheless, recent operations have highlighted serious shortcomings in these 5 areas. Although existing executive branch authority will enable many solutions, other challenges will require changes to the law necessitating that Congress act as it did with the Goldwater-Nichols Act of 1986, which mandated a sweeping reorganization of the DoD. Currently, however, Congress lacks the relevant institutional mechanisms and perhaps the political will for doing so. Skeptics may be concerned that Capitol Hill will never undertake comprehensive national security reform, but in asserting this, they ignore the case of Goldwater-Nichols, which was passed over bitter opposition by the DoD.

The example of Goldwater-Nichols provides hope for congressional action on national security reform, but admittedly, there are important differences between it and today's reorganization needs. First, the contemporary security threat environment is much more complex and rapidly changing than that of the 1980s. Modern challenges require approaches that are not purely diplomatic, developmental, or defensive in nature, often demanding tools that cross agency lines. This reality presents challenges of jurisdiction, authorization, and appropriations that will require a more intricate organizational practice than that instituted in the Goldwater-Nichols era.

Second, the scope of national security reform necessary is unprecedented in its size and complexity and may be 15-20 times bigger than Goldwater-Nichols. Those who have studied PNSR's work have noted that there has never been a transformation effort as large as that currently being attempted. While Goldwater-Nichols addressed only the DoD, the current reform must include the entire national security system, both in the executive and legislative branches. Furthermore, today's reform will have to consider international and domestic security apparatuses, encompassing organizations not considered under Goldwater-Nichols to include state, local, tribal, and territorial governments as well as nongovernmental and private organizations.

Third, in addition to broad changes to existing institutions, national security reform necessitates the creation of entirely new entities and capacities, a challenge not tackled in Goldwater-Nichols, which only provided the proper authorities to already-existing organizations.[2] The creation of these new entities will demand a concentrated effort by both the executive and legislative branches.

Finally, the scope of national security reform demands careful stewardship through and by Congress. However, whereas Goldwater-Nichols benefited from ownership by the Senate and House Armed Services Committees, no one committee sees itself as having the mandate to push for current reform initiatives. The absence of a congressional champion has stymied the progress of national security reform on Capitol Hill. Furthermore, today's Congress is constrained by partisan political considerations, which has prevented a truly bipartisan approach. Bipartisanship was crucial to the ultimate success of Goldwater-Nichols. Republican Senator Barry Goldwater and Democratic Senator Sam Nunn demonstrated tremendous skill in forging this legislation and ushering it through a Republican Senate and a Democratic House.

Indeed, the challenges of national security reform on Capitol Hill are formidable and multifaceted, encompassing intellectual, political, scope, ownership, and bandwidth challenges. Intellectually, because the legislature lacks jurisdiction and the institutional mechanisms to systematically look at interagency issues, it does not have the requisite storehouse of knowledge. As it did with Goldwater-Nichols, when Capitol Hill knew little about defense institutions, Congress will have to devote time and resources to understanding interagency organizational practice. In addition to this intellectual challenge, politically entrenched congressional interests favor the status quo and discourage comprehensive reform. Furthermore, with multiple stakeholders involved and the complexity of reform required, the scope of reorganization is simply daunting, inhibiting congressional engagement and commitment. The compounding of these challenges, and the amount of time reform will demand, create a bandwidth challenge; Goldwater-Nichols took 4 years and 241 days to enact, and in order to achieve success, the Act was the top priority of the Senate Armed Services Committee for 2 years. Nearly 2-and-a-half decades on, as the inefficiencies of the congressional process have grown, finding the capacity on Capitol Hill to undertake institutional reform on the scale of today's requirements has become more challenging.

Certainly, the task of national security reform is significant, demanding a focused, bipartisan effort in both the executive and legislative branches. While today's transformation will prove a more demanding effort than the Goldwater-Nichols Act, the experience of the 1980s proved that seemingly insurmountable challenges can be overcome with skillfulness and commitment. Modern national security reform is not a novel preoccupation; it is essential to the national interest of the United States, and Congress must act to make it a reality.

ENDNOTES - CHAPTER 4

1. Project on National Security Reform (PNSR), *Turning Ideas into Action*, Arlington, VA: PNSR, 2008, pp. 404-434, available from *www.pnsr.org/data/files/pnsr_turning_ideas_into_action.pdf*.

2. "Goldwater-Nichols Department of Defense Reorganization Act of 1986," Washington, DC: U.S. Government Printing Office, 1986, available from *www.au.af.mil/au/awc/awcgate/congress/title_10.htm*.

CHAPTER 5

CONGRESSIONAL NATIONAL SECURITY REFORM:
A MID-OBAMA ADMINISTRATION REVIEW

Richard Weitz

The Project on National Security Reform (PNSR) is comprised of former senior national security executives and military leaders, as well as foreign affairs, international development, and human capital experts. Since 2007, this bipartisan group has engaged in an intensive analysis of the U.S. national security system, with particular attention to the interagency aspects of national security. It is the perhaps the premier organization on issues relating to national security reform, the topic that is PNSR's exclusive focus.

The PNSR offered a vision for the national security system of the 21st century in its November 2008 report, *Forging a New Shield.*[1] This report offers the most comprehensive study of the U.S. national security system in American history. Its vision stresses the need for holistic reform, as contrasted to the piecemeal reform that has been pursued since 1947. This new improved national security system would:

- employ whole-of-government approaches;
- operate effectively across the interagency;
- reflect the insights and innovations that come from collaboration by many varied perspectives, both inside and outside government;
- empower leaders to make timely, informed decisions and take decisive action;
- be sufficiently cohesive and agile both to seize opportunities and overcome threats;

- ensure that the national security system integrates all elements of national power and puts mission outcomes first;
- coordinate effectively between the federal government and state, local, tribal, and territorial governments and other mission partners.

To realize this vision of a collaborative, agile, and innovative national security system that horizontally and vertically integrates all elements of national power, the PNSR develops several key concepts for processes that would improve U.S. national security decisionmaking: strategic management, effective resource allocation, empowered interagency teams, a dedicated national security workforce, and a collaborative culture of information sharing. In *Toward Integrating Complex International Missions*, the PNSR sought to document the lessons it learned from supporting the National Counterterrorism Center's Directorate of Strategic Operational Planning.[2]

In the fall of 2009, the PNSR published another report, *Turning Ideas into Action*. This document reiterates and refines the recommendations in *Forging a New Shield*. It also outlines specific next steps that must be undertaken by the American government to implement systemic transformation. The report found that reform is underway and that progress is being made toward a national security system able to respond more effectively to 21st-century challenges and opportunities.[3] President Barack Obama is a consistent advocate of U.S. national security reform. He and others in the administration have spoken of the complex challenges facing the United States and the need for change. Nonetheless, major problems with the U.S. national security system remain. Policy formation and execution is still stovepiped by department and agency lanes rather than a result of a genuinely integrated, horizontal interagency collaboration. The system continues to lack unity of purpose and strategic direction, partly because strategy and resources are not aligned. Furthermore, policymakers do not routinely consider all elements of national power in decisions and strategies. Finally, Congress still lacks the proper structure to exercise oversight of interagency activities.

THE CONGRESSIONAL IMPERATIVE

Congress has a major role in reforming the national security organizations and processes in the executive branch. Since its establishment, the PNSR has devoted substantial attention to Congress in recognition of the crucial importance of the legislative branch in shaping U.S. national security strategy. The Project first sought to determine the current role of Congress and its various committees in supporting and overseeing the national security system. PNSR analysts therefore undertook a comprehensive review of recent studies of these issues, including those by the Government Accountability Office and internal department and agency inspectors general. The PNSR then recommended congressional and other oversight changes consistent with the organizational strategy, structure, processes, and personnel recommendations made by its other working groups. The specific methodology was to:

- Examine the history and underlying assumptions of the current congressional oversight mechanisms and procedures to determine how they took their current form;

- Identify recurring problems, their causes, and their consequences;
- Explain how core problems differ from peripheral ones;
- Isolate critical impediments to success;
- Develop the full range of alternative solutions;
- Evaluate alternative solutions;
- Make appropriate recommendations; and,
- Identify practical means to ensure successful implementation of the recommended reforms.

The PNSR made two core assumptions when examining Congress. First, that the congressional leadership would support adjustments to the body's committee structure and other oversight mechanisms in order to improve overall national security. Second, that the Congress would support legal and procedural reforms to improve executive branch national security performance in the context of an overarching reform effort.

Forging a New Shield identified six problems that impede the contribution of Congress to U.S. national security policy:[4]

1. There is no routine oversight of interagency issues, operations, or requirements.

2. Congress lacks interest and confidence in the executive branch's management of foreign affairs.

3. The overall allocation of resources between all elements of national power, including defense, diplomacy, and development, tends toward inflexibility.

4. A slow confirmation process for presidential appointees leads to inaction and bureaucratic drift on many issues.

5. Failure to pass timely legislation has become endemic.

6. Legislative and executive branches have lost the ability to work together productively.

The PNSR then offered a series of recommendations to address these problems.

STRATEGY DEVELOPMENT AND PLANNING GUIDANCE

In both reports and in other documents, the PNSR calls for developing a national security strategy and accompanying planning and resource guidance for the interagency system. *Turning Ideas Into Action* concluded that establishing a permanent strategy directorate in the National Security Staff could strengthen strategy development. The directorate would set direction and advance objectives to ensure the government is prepared to address near-, medium-, and long-term challenges as well as capitalize on new opportunities. To fulfill these objectives, the strategy directorate should produce three documents for presidential approval:

1. A *National Security Review* (NSR) to assess strategic challenges and capabilities;

2. A *National Security Strategy* (NSS) to focus the executive branch; and,

3. A *National Security Planning and Resource Guidance* (NSPRG) to implement and fund the strategy.

The NSR would establish the administration's strategy baseline for decisionmaking. It would guide senior strategists and policy planners from across the national security interagency system as well as other government stakeholders and experts. The NSR's specific objectives would be:

- To describe the strategic landscape;
- To assess existing capabilities and resources against needs;
- To make recommendations regarding missions, activities, and budgets;
- To review the scope and assumptions of national security, including possible changes in roles and responsibilities within the interagency and among external stakeholders; and,
- To occur on a quadrennial cycle, preceding and informing departmental reviews, with annual updates.

The NSR would be used to craft the administration's NSS, which would comprise a political document in narrative form that would establish the President's national security objectives by region and transnational issue. The NSS's specific objectives would be to identify significant challenges in the international and domestic security environment and their implications for homeland security policy. The NSS would be published once during each presidential term in order to establish the administration's prioritized national security objectives as well as its criteria to manage risks and opportunities, given available resources.[5]

The NSPRG would translate the President's NSS into policy, planning, and resource guidance to departments and agencies. Specifically, the NSPRG would provide annually updated 6-year resource profiles covering the capabilities of each department and agency for meeting future national security needs as defined in the NSS. As part of this process, the National Security Staff and the Office of Management of Budget (OMB) would jointly issue this resource guidance at the beginning of the annual program and budgeting cycle. A copy of the annual resource guidance would be provided to Congress to help inform the authorization and appropriation processes.

The strategy reviews under the Obama administration have indeed been very inclusive. These reviews include the drafting of a new *Quadrennial Defense Review* (QDR), *Nuclear Posture Review, Ballistic Missile Defense Review*, and the most recently released NSS. They all employed a whole-of-government approach in which the National Security Council (NSC) solicited advice and input from across the national security community. The reviews themselves stressed the need to improve interagency cooperation as well as develop and use all elements of American national power, not just the military. For example, the 2010 QDR stresses the need to institutionalize greater "partnership capacity" across all Department of Defense (DoD) areas.[6] This effort lends itself to greater interagency coordination between the military component of national power and the remaining components, such as diplomacy, intelligence, and economy (development).

Congressional legislation contributed to this process. The Foreign Relations Authorization Act of 2009 mandated a State Department review of diplomacy and development. In addition to identifying key objectives and missions for U.S. foreign policy and assistance, it calls for an interagency approach to strategy:

> Each Quadrennial Review of Diplomacy and Development shall take into account the views of the Secretary of State, the Administrator of the United States Agency for International Development, the Secretary of Defense, the Secretary of the Treasury, the United States Trade Representative, and the head of any other relevant agency.[7]

The House Foreign Affairs Committee also introduced the Foreign Relations Authorization Act for Fiscal Years 2010 and 2011 (H.R. 2410) mandating a *Quadrennial Diplomacy and Development Review*.[8] Various members of Congress, including U.S. Representative Jim Langevin (D-RI), have introduced bills requiring a *Quadrennial National Security Review* (QNSR) with the objective of establishing overarching goals to create unity of purpose among departments and agencies pursuing national security objectives. For example, H.R. 4974 states that:

> The President shall, in consultation with the Director of the Office of Management and Budget, Congress, and the heads of other appropriate departments and agencies responsible for national security, conduct a quadrennial national security review . . . to set forth the security goals, including long-term and short-term security goals, of the United States.[9]

This year has seen an unprecedented number of narrower reviews, including the *Quadrennial Defense Review*, *Quadrennial Homeland Security Review*, *Quadrennial Intelligence Community Review*, and *Quadrennial Diplomacy and Development Review*. This bill would integrate these efforts and institutionalize a whole-of-government approach to setting U.S. national security priorities. Producing an interagency *National Security Review* every 4 years will be a significant step along the path of national security reform by providing the whole government, including Congress, a common strategy to guide planning and resource allocation across departments and agencies.

INTERAGENCY TEAMS AND TASK FORCES

The PNSR has sought to delegate and unify management of national security issues and missions through empowered interagency teams and crisis task forces. Although U.S. national security missions are shifting, broadening, and becoming increasingly interdisciplinary, the current national security system, encumbered by inflexible stovepipes, needs further reform to meet today's multidimensional national security challenges. The recommendations made in *Forging a New Shield* stressed the importance of employing an interagency team approach to issue and mission management. The goal was to rectify the problems posed by overly centralized decision making, insufficient guidance for and coordination of policy implementation, and insufficient linkage of authorities to mission demands. These recommendations encompass system-wide changes, as well as their enabling mechanisms.

With congressional support, the Obama administration has developed several interagency teams with wide executive branch representation for important geographic areas, including Afghanistan-Pakistan and the Sudan. The PNSR had the privilege of being able to provide direct support to the latter team, which is led by the U.S. Special Envoy to Sudan (USSES). The PNSR helped establish the USSES as an empowered interagency team that employed a whole-of-government approach in order to develop a holistic and integrated U.S. approach to the situation in Sudan. Unfortunately, although the PNSR believes in the potential for the USSES to act as a model for applying a PNSR-designed interagency team approach to other priority national security issues currently being managed by czars and special envoys, the interagency team model has yet to be extended across the U.S. Government through either executive or congressional branch action.

ALIGNED STRATEGY AND RESOURCES

Linking resources to goals through national security mission-based analysis and resourcing is essential for making progress on congressional reform. National security executives must be able to link resources to strategic goals, because aligning national security strategy with resources is essential. For a plan to be genuinely strategic, it must account for both the capabilities and the costs of implementation. National security reforms must empower policymakers to set strategic objectives and obtain the means to achieve them. Resource allocation reform is critical for addressing complex security threats, major emergencies, and opportunities. Linking national security priorities and budgets would allow policymakers to make improved decisions across the entire national security system and provide a capability to respond better to the security challenges and opportunities that arise. These reforms would greatly enhance U.S. national security, help eliminate waste, and more efficiently allocate resources.

Past PNSR research has identified three core problems regarding resource management. First, strategy and policy priorities do not drive resource allocation and tradeoffs. Second, the national security system is unable to resource the full range of required capabilities for national priority missions. Third, it is difficult to provide resources for crises requiring an urgent interagency response.[10]

In the current system, national security funding is distributed program by program, department by department, agency by agency. The resource allocation process focuses on means rather than ends and relies on policy entrepreneurs within the interagency to work around bureaucratic impediments to achieve successful mission outcomes. Other problems contribute to these larger flaws. First is the absence of an agreement on which parts of an agency budget should be included in an integrated national security budget. Another is that national security departments and agencies differ considerably in terms of program/budget calendars, resource displays/formats, and planning horizons (e.g., DoD, the Department of Homeland Security [DHS] and the Intelligence Community use 5-6 years, but other agencies typically consider only 1-2 years). As a result of these problems, departments and agencies typically shortchange interagency missions and nontraditional capabilities. In addition, the requirements for national mission success are often not met. In particular, the resource allocation processes do not provide the full range of required capabilities, do not permit the system to surge in response to priority needs, and do not provide resource allocation flexibility in response to changing circumstances.[11]

The existing national security strategy development and resource allocation system is largely a relic of the Cold War. It is clearly inadequate for meeting today's complex and fast-breaking security challenges. The U.S. federal budgeting model follows a process that predates the American colonies. The legislature appropriates funds, while the executive expends them according to congressional specifications. During the past 2 centuries, however, the role of the President and his staff has grown substantially. The process has also become more complex. At any time, the federal budgets for 3 fiscal years are simultaneously under consideration. Historically, departments and agencies prepare their own budget requests each summer with guidance from the OMB. The President and OMB review the requests, make final decisions, and submit a consolidated budget request to Congress. Congress reviews the requests and appropriates funds, sometimes with accompanying authorizing legislation. The executive branch then executes the functions for which monies are appropriated.

From the late 1940s through the end of the Cold War, the resource allocation system for national security consisted largely of forming and reviewing the defense and intelligence budgets. At the time, this process may have been appropriate, since most national security funding, including intelligence funding, resided in the DoD budget. Starting in the early 1990s, and especially since 2001, the growing complexity of potential threats and the importance of interagency cooperation for accomplishing national security missions have exposed systemic weaknesses in the traditional resource allocation system. In particular, serious problems exist regarding national strategy development as well as aligning resources with strategy, which requires cross-agency resource allocation:

- Departments and agencies formulate budget requests to support their own programs.
- National strategy and contingency funding are not primary considerations.
- This orientation makes it difficult to assess whether budgets will support strategy.
- It also can mislead officials into thinking that they can carry out policies when insufficient funds have been provided.

- Not all decisions need initial budgetary inputs, but they eventually must be considered to prevent policy failure.
- Furthermore, the current process of mediating agency budget requests after formulation does not effectively address contingencies that require integrated interagency action.
- Existing processes for moving funds between agencies with national security responsibilities are generally cumbersome and inefficient; even redirecting unspent funds to other agencies to address urgent contingencies is difficult.
- As a result, crosscutting programs that address complex or urgent threats often do not receive adequate or timely funding.

Resolving these problems requires directing each national security department and agency to prepare a 6-year budget projection derived from the proposed NSPRG. The President should direct the National Security Staff's strategy directorate, in partnership with the OMB Office of National Security Programs, to produce and disseminate annual policy planning and resource guidance to departments and agencies, including guidance concerning necessary capabilities to be developed for current and future needs. The resource guidance should provide annually updated 6-year resource profiles covering each department/agency's capabilities for meeting future national security needs, as suggested by the NSR and as defined in the NSS. The NSPRG direction would provide annual policy planning and resource guidance. These documents would be disseminated to departments and agencies with national security roles and missions, but also to the appropriate congressional committees. This reform would help ensure more realistic annual budget requests from departments and agencies, thus enhancing mission preparedness, reducing waste, and enabling more effective contingency response.

Congress also needs to develop the capability to produce an integrated national security budget. One metric would be a unified budget focused around national security missions that would shift resources to a whole-of-government approach. An integrated national security budget presentation to Congress would improve funding of national security mission priorities and reconcile resource imbalances among agencies. Moreover, it would provide a clear vision of how to resource missions requiring the participation of multiple agencies. It should be derived from the NSR process and the NSS, and, through the President's budget submission to Congress, provide a single integrated national security budget display along with integrated budget justification material that reflects how each department's and each agency's budget aligns with underlying security assessments, strategy, and resource guidance.

The PNSR would like Congress to contribute to this resource reform effort by establishing select committees on national security in the House and Senate that would have jurisdiction over interagency operations and activities. Congressional committees organized along departmental equities reinforce departmental and agency tendencies to protect turf and power rather than reconcile imbalances. One effect is that well-funded departments, like the DoD, inevitably are called to assume the responsibilities of other, underfunded, nonmilitary agencies like the Department of State. Pending the creation of select national security committees, executive-legislative consultations could encourage the House and Senate Budget Committees to consider an integrated national security budget in addition to the customary component-specific authorizations.

Congress also needs to reform the existing inadequate portfolio of contingency funding mechanisms to address emerging threats and situations that demand urgent interagency responses. The current resource allocation system is unable to address the full range of capabilities required for key national missions. Instead, it actively discourages departments and agencies from budgeting for external or contingent purposes, even for national security. Rightfully concerned about maintaining its power of the purse, Congress has historically resisted allocating contingency funds. Various congressional limits on reprogramming and transfer authority complicate or limit sufficient response when contingencies actually emerge. Congress should develop new accounts and procedures to meet unanticipated requirements that necessitate an integrated interagency approach. For example, Congress should consider establishing a mechanism for expedited fund transfers between agencies for contingencies that require interagency integration. An integrated national security budget presentation and executive-legislative consultations on the subject could advance this effort.

HOMELAND SECURITY MISSION INTEGRATION AND COORDINATION

The PNSR urges the creation of a homeland security and emergency management system that integrates federal, state, local, territorial, and tribal interests. The currently fragmented national security and homeland security structures leave us vulnerable to both natural and manmade disasters. For most of the nation's history, national security threats against the homeland have originated outside U.S. borders and involved only the federal level of government. Today, national security threats transcend this division, requiring that state and local entities possess the ability to integrate and communicate up to the national level to address all potential hazards, from natural disasters to terrorist attacks to catastrophic accidents such as in the Gulf of Mexico [the 2010 Gulf oil rig disaster]. The transforming security landscape also requires that the federal security apparatus provide the organizational conduits, processes, resources, and planning guidance to allow that linkage when appropriate, both constitutionally and as homeland emergency operations dictate.

The DHS has made some progress in this direction by conducting the first *Quadrennial Homeland Security Review*. The next step would be to develop a *National Operational Framework* (NOF) to better address homeland security challenges. The NOF would provide a primary means for reconciling homeland security's integrated policy and planning efforts within an operational structure. It would encompass the entire homeland security mission continuum, easing confusion throughout the interagency and intergovernmental systems while enabling a closer working relationship among all stakeholder — both public and private.

The PNSR also recommends complementary systemic reform at the regional level to strengthen the National Preparedness System (NPS), which was defined by the Post Katrina Emergency Management Reform Act (PKEMRA) of 2006. The PNSR white paper, "Recalibrating the System: Toward Efficient and Effective

Resourcing of National Preparedness," cites fundamental and interrelated structural and process problems plaguing the current system.[12] It recommends direct funding from the federal government—instead of
resourcing through grants—for national catastrophic
planning and assessments. Resourcing primarily via
grants, with their oversight and reporting requirements, fosters intergovernmental relationships that
can be more adversarial than collaborative and thus
not optimal for unity of purpose. The study recommends that the DHS and the Federal Emergency Management Agency (FEMA) finance an intergovernmental, interagency Regional Catastrophic Preparedness
Staff (RCPS) in each region. These standing regional
staffs would be where federal, state, tribal, territorial,
local, private sector, and nongovernmental organization (NGO) representatives would come together
daily, from the beginning, as equal partners to build a
bottom-up, collaborative culture of preparedness—or
even resilience—and the collaborative regional programs to go with it. This initiative would not impose
a financial burden on the states or localities. The state
and local authorities would assign representatives to
an RCPS for temporary duty and receive federal re-
imbursements under the Intergovernmental Personnel Act (IPA) Mobility program. Since it is only at the
regional level where we can arrive at a consensus for
that region, standing RCPSs would work with existing
planning, training, and exercise units in the states and
at the local level to conduct catastrophic risk assessments; catastrophic operational planning and exercise
validation; catastrophic capability inventories via ne-
gotiated processes through which states could identify gaps for targeting grants and other resources; and
regional evaluations and self-assessments informed
by regionally determined performance metrics.

HUMAN CAPITAL

The PNSR calls for developing a national security strategic human capital plan to align human capital programs with strategic goals, objectives, and outcomes. *Forging a New Shield* found that, "The [current] national security system cannot generate or allocate the personnel necessary to perform effectively and efficiently agency core tasks or the growing number of important interagency tasks."[13] A well-designed and executed human capital system for the national security mission will help attract, retain, promote, reward, and educate a capable workforce to advance and defend the United States. The current system and its associated human capital policies, programs, procedures, and incentives are unable to generate the required human capital with the requisite competencies to ensure a continuing supply of well-qualified national security personnel. It also cannot assign the right people, with the right competencies, at the right time, to execute interagency tasks successfully. Furthermore, the current national security system cannot overcome the historic dominance of several strong department and agency cultures. It also does not ensure that political and career officials pay sufficient attention to building the human resource capacity needed to achieve interagency missions and priorities, especially when those might conflict with the missions and priorities of individual departments and agencies. Continuous learning is essential for a well-qualified national security workforce; it requires increasing opportunities for education, training, and professional development. Providing a system for interagency assignments is also essential for ensuring that national security professionals have practical experience in interagency work.

Yet, developing a successful interagency assignment process will prove particularly complex, since it requires identifying core competencies for national security work; determining assignments that will build those competencies; establishing an administrative system to match people with assignments; identifying or creating an organization to provide policy, management, and oversight for the process; and providing the positions, funds, and coordinating mechanisms required for an interagency assignment system to operate effectively.

The government's newly created National Security Professional Development Integration Office (the NSPD-IO) represents an important first step toward the creation of national security executives. It was established by Executive Order 13434 on May 17, 2007, and has already developed and promulgated the *National Strategy for the Development of Security Professionals*; provided OPM guidance for developing promotion regulations and additional authorizations; created the National Security Professional Development Integration Office; and established a National Security Education and Training Board of Directors. Furthermore, the NSPD-IO has identified approximately 1,500 Senior Executive Service (SES) positions with national security responsibilities; created an education council that has agreed on certain general standards; encouraged existing departments and agencies to establish education and training programs for national security professionals; and designed and made available system-wide courses. The NSPD-IO's Defense Senior Leader Development Program (DSLDP), the management program for DoD's SESs, has improved with National Security Professional Development initiatives as well as the OPM's Executive Core Qualifications (ECQ). These reforms have helped promote an "enterprise-wide perspective" that features strategic, top-level understanding of individual and organizational responsibilities and strategic priorities.[14]

The Office of the Director of National Intelligence (ODNI) has also implemented an award-winning Intelligence Community Civilian Joint Duty program that fosters interagency collaboration and communication. The ODNI Intelligence Community Civilian Joint Duty Program was adopted on June 25, 2007, with phased implementation to be complete by October 2010. In September 2008, the IC (Intelligence Community) Joint Duty Program received the "Innovations in American Government" award by the Ash Institute of Harvard University's Kennedy School of Government. The ODNI has issued policies and procedures for performance assessment and promotion that support interagency assignments within the IC, the appropriate sharing of information between and among intelligence agencies, and assurance that interagency assignments would be viewed positively when considering IC employees for promotion.[15]

The NSPD-IO and ODNI initiatives are encouraging, since they indicate that it is possible to establish certain system-wide performance requirements. The experience of the DoD joint assignment process, recent NSPD-IO and ODNI initiatives, and emerging insights from several PNSR initiatives suggest that properly designed and executed pilot programs are particularly effective in confirming what works and identifying unintended consequences of new policies and procedures. Furthermore, it is evident that interagency assignments are beginning to be seen as contributing to an employee's growth and development. Yet, these activities remain largely managed within the cultural stovepipes of the individual departments and agencies. The essential next step is to create an interagency culture within the larger national security community. In this regard, while the DoD's Goldwater-Nichols experience provides useful insights into broad reform frameworks, substantial differences exist between the military human capital system (e.g., up-or-out promotion system, established expectation of multiple assignments, the Uniform Code of Military Justice to compel acceptance of assignments, etc.) and current civilian human capital systems.

The PNSR has also recommended that the Congress should strengthen education and training programs for interagency personnel by creating a comprehensive, professional education and training program with an interdisciplinary curriculum. The Congress must provide additional revenue to enlarge the civilian workforce to create a "float" that will enable interagency training, education, and experiential opportunities. A mandatory orientation program would be required for each individual assigned to a national security position. The Congress should give high priority to preparing civilian personnel for leadership positions in the national security system. It should also require individuals appointed to serve in high-level national security positions to complete a structured orientation on the policy and operations of the national security interagency system. The Congress should authorize and fund an executive office to support development and execution of the above reforms and provide continuing policy determinations and oversight for interagency national security human capital programs.

In any case, successful implementation of any reform will depend, in part, on codifying existing human capital systems. To achieve coherence and optimal performance in a reformed interagency human capital system, moreover, an enhanced management function is required. Further consultations with stakeholders and subject matter experts will clarify the extent of legislation required to ensure continuity in interagency management. Nonetheless, the following questions should be answered before proceeding to implement any specific reform:

- What defines the aggregate national security interagency system, its workforce, and its key component parts, such as the National Security Professional Corps?
- What costs arise from establishing the interagency human capital system? What are the estimated number of positions? What is the definition of the national security professional corps? How many people would that comprise?
- What are the potential benefits and costs? How will both be measured?
- What specific goals or purposes will interagency rotational assignments achieve? How will the costs and benefits of such a program be measured?
- What types of positions and organizations constitute or contribute to the national security interagency system?
- How will interagency assignments be identified? How will national security professionals be identified and assigned to these positions?
- How do we avoid the present need to provide so much detail that laws or executive orders prove inadequate to address needs that could easily evolve within the next 5-to-10 years?

Regardless of which specific reforms the ODNI, White House, and the Congress support, the executive and legislative branches should partner to require the periodic review of the National Security Strategic Human Capital Plan. They should also approve a human capital advisory board of public and private experts to advise the appropriate officials of the national security staff; and establish new interagency personnel designations and programs to better recruit, prepare, and reward national security professionals for interagency assignments.

KNOWLEDGE AND INTELLECTUAL CAPITAL

A well-functioning U.S. national security system requires a great improvement in the flow of knowledge and information among national security decisionmakers. Today the national security system "does not know what it knows." Both within individual government agencies and across the broader interagency environment, the tools and willingness to share are sorely lacking. Technology to share data is not readily available; policies and procedures promote an attitude that information is something that is "owned" rather than something to be shared; and government employees fear that exchanging "too much" information can hurt someone's career. As a result, data producers do not make their holdings known or discoverable, while data consumers have no idea what might exist to help them. Requirements for security clearances and information classification policies vary widely from agency to agency. In addition, time-sensitive information is often conveyed by fax machine, and agencies' computer systems are often incompatible with those in other agencies.

The PNSR supports the set of recommendations offered in the Markle Foundation's *Nation at Risk: Policy Makers Need Better Information to Protect the Country.*

They cover the full range of technological, procedural, structural, and cultural challenges that must be addressed before the U.S. national security system can make knowledge- and information-sharing a reality. The core Markle recommendations are: reaffirm information sharing as a top priority; make government information discoverable and accessible to authorized users; enhance security and privacy protections to match the increased power of shared information; transform the information-sharing culture with metrics and incentives; and empower users to drive information sharing by forming communities of interest.[16]

Adopting these recommendations should help ensure that what an organization knows can be captured, leveraged, and exchanged for the benefit of all authorized and authenticated members of the national security community. The ultimate objective is to make decisions that are better, faster, and more likely to achieve decisive action. Intelligent information-sharing must become the norm, as national security decisionmakers shift from "need to know" to "need to share."

It is important to recognize that technology alone will not solve the problem of inadequate knowledge- and information-sharing within the U.S. national security system. It must be complemented by an information-sharing culture that extends throughout the greater national security community. The national security system must capture, leverage, and exchange data, information, and knowledge more effectively. People can then make better decisions more rapidly — leading to more decisive policy development and execution. Furthermore, the mindset of national security members must change from a culture that is too risk averse. National security policymakers must manage risks rather than avoid every possible hazard.

IMPROVING CONGRESSIONAL OVERSIGHT

None of these reforms can be comprehensively implemented or achieve a sustained improvement in national security decisionmaking without an improvement in how Congress oversees the system. In its oversight role, Congress has a responsibility to promote efficiency, economy, effectiveness, responsiveness, and accountability. When performed well, congressional oversight ensures compliance with the laws passed by Congress and the orders issued under the authority of the President. It can also assess the effectiveness and efficiency of government programs and provide senior officials with alternate sources of information about the performance of subordinate personnel and organizations. Congressional oversight can expose problems, provide incentives for solutions, stimulate good performance, and deter misconduct. Furthermore, congressional oversight can help ensure accountability and consistency with America's goals, values, and laws.

Forging a New Shield identified six major problems in congressional performance in national security affairs. First, Congress does not provide routine oversight of interagency issues, operations, or requirements. Second, Congress lacks interest and confidence in the executive branch's management of foreign affairs. Third, Congress needs to offer more flexibility in how it allocates national security resources. Fourth, Congress must accelerate the process of confirming presidential appointees to reduce the extent of inaction and bureaucratic drift among national security decisionmakers. Fifth, Congress's failure to enact legislation in a timely manner has become endemic. Finally, relations between the legislative and executive branches are too often excessively confrontational despite the importance of achieving cooperation regarding national security issues.

The PNSR is not unique in citing these problems with congressional oversight. Earlier blue-ribbon commissions and other analysts point to structural inadequacies in the committee system, they complain about the neglect of important issues, and they lament both qualitative and quantitative shortfalls in congressional oversight. For example, the Hart-Rudman Commission criticized the executive branch for "often treat[ing] Congress as an obstacle rather than as a partner," and blamed Congress for "sustain[ing] a structure that undermines rather than strengthens its ability to fulfill its constitutional obligations in the foreign policy arena."[17] The 9/11 (September 11, 2001) Commission declared that "Congressional oversight for intelligence—and counterterrorism – is now dysfunctional."[18] The Center for Strategic and International Studies (CSIS) *Beyond Goldwater-Nichols* project report said that after consulting numerous current and former officials in both branches of government, "Practically all agree that there has been a significant and disturbing degree of erosion in the quality and structure of congressional oversight of the [Defense] Department in recent years."[19] These criticisms are consistent with the broader studies of congressional oversight that usually conclude that either little or no oversight is done, or "when done that it is uncoordinated, unsystematic, sporadic, and usually informal, with members of Congress (or groups of members on narrowly based committee units) seeking particularistic influence or publicity for purposes of reelection."[20]

Members of Congress presently struggle to see the big-picture interrelationship among all elements of national power. Congressional leadership tolerates a Congress that cannot authorize, finance, or oversee the interagency approaches envisioned by executive branch leaders and the preceding recommendations in this report. Instead of structuring itself to catalyze the interagency approaches envisioned and required by the executive branch, the Congress in fact reinforces outdated, department-centric practices. The existing committees in Congress examine the activities of individual departments and agencies, but no one congressional committee has a whole-of-government perspective on national security. Perhaps for this reason, the Congress is not keeping up with the rapid changes in the executive branch. To take but one example, the Obama administration's National Security Council combines homeland security, economic security, and transnational security issues, such as climate change, within the NSC portfolio, but the Congress lacks a means to address these issues in a similarly integrated manner.

Eight congressional committees, one each in the House and Senate, have significant oversight jurisdiction for national security matters: the foreign policy, defense, intelligence, and appropriations committees. In addition, however, many other committees handle issues that have national security aspects. For example, the tax committees (House Ways & Means, Senate Finance) have jurisdiction over trade legislation and agreements, while export controls and import controls are handled by different committees in each body. No single committee is responsible for overseeing the interagency process for national security or the broad policy issues and legal authorities for the Executive

Office of the President or the National Security Council. Reorganization proposals are the responsibility of the Government Affairs/Government Reform committees but thereafter the various departmentally-focused committees have jurisdiction. The foreign policy committees have broad jurisdiction over relations with other countries and "intervention abroad and declarations of war" (House Rule X and Senate Rule XXV have identical language on this point), while the defense committees are vaguely limited to the DoD and "common defense" issues. Since 1977, the Senate Foreign Relations Committee has had a special mandate to "study and review, on a comprehensive basis, matters relating to the national security policy, foreign policy, and international economic policy as it relates to the foreign policy of the United States."[21] Its House counterpart has no similar mandate.

The defense committees have reported annual authorization bills since the 1960s. These measures now cover all areas included in the regular defense appropriations bill. The foreign policy committees try to pass authorizations for the State Department, but no foreign aid authorization bill has been enacted since 1986. As a consequence, international affairs programs and legislation are now largely influenced by the appropriations subcommittees and included in their bills. Intelligence activities are overseen by the Senate Select Committee on Intelligence and the House Permanent Select Committee on Intelligence, which develop an annual authorization bill covering most, but not all, programs. The remaining so-called tactical intelligence activities for the armed forces are handled by the defense authorizing committees. The DHS faces a very complicated situation, with 86 congressional subcommittees having jurisdiction over some DHS programs. In addition to the two standing committees having departmental oversight, numerous other panels have legacy oversight of programs—like customs and the Coast Guard—that have responsibilities in addition to homeland security. Foreign economic policy matters, which often have major national security aspects or consequences, are fragmented among a wide array of congressional committees. Trade committees oversee trade and tariff questions. The foreign policy committees oversee foreign aid, the international financial institutions, and the foreign policy aspects of economic relations. Export controls are handled by the Banking Committee in the Senate and the Foreign Affairs Committee in the House. Agricultural imports and exports are under the agriculture committees. Import quotas can be voted by the Commerce, Interior, and environmental committees. Appropriations are handled by 12 subcommittees, each reporting a separate bill. Defense spending is largely covered by the defense appropriations bill and subcommittees, except for military construction funds that are included with veterans programs. Foreign operations funding, including foreign aid, is now part of a money bill for the State Department and international organizations. Department of State funds until 2006 competed with the Commerce and Justice Departments in a multiagency bill and subcommittee. Funds for the President and the NSC are appropriated through the Financial Services and General Government funding bill. Reorganization issues are the purview of the Senate Homeland Security and Governmental Affairs Committee and the House Committee on Oversight and Government Reform. A separate House standing committee oversees the DHS. The House committee has a subcommittee on National Security and Foreign Affairs, but the Senate panel includes the subject under its subcommittee on

Federal Financial Management, Government Information, Federal Services, and International Security. As a result, formal jurisdiction over interagency operations is limited to issues relating to government reorganization rather than oversight of ongoing activities.

In addition to oversight activities by congressional committees, there are several other venues for oversight. The most active is the Government Accountability Office (GAO), which regularly reviews and investigates government programs, partly on its own initiative and partly in response to congressional requests. Other agents of the legislative branch are the Congressional Budget Office (CBO), which analyzes programs in terms of their costs and alternatives, and the Congressional Research Service (CSR), which prepares reports on topics of current interest to lawmakers. Congress has also created Inspector General (IG) offices within major departments and with some degree of independence from political appointee control. In addition, Congress has mandated periodic review of some national security policies through the *Quadrennial Defense Review* (QDR) and has, on occasion, created outside panels—like the National Defense Panel and Hart-Rudman Commission—for independent assessments. Presidents also use permanent or temporary groups to review and report on agency activities. Examples include the President's Foreign Intelligence Advisory Board (PFIAB) and panels like the Iraq Study Group.

MEETING THE CONGRESSIONAL IMPERATIVE

The PNSR wants—indeed, insists on—an important congressional role in making and overseeing national security policy. To this end, the PNSR earlier recommended establishing select committees on national security in the Senate and House of Representatives. These new committees would authorize and oversee programs and activities that are conducted by multiple departments and agencies in support of national security and foreign relations missions. These committees would draw their membership from the standing defense, foreign relations, and reformed homeland security committees, as well as other committees with jurisdiction over national security and foreign relations. Their creation would help achieve a number of other goals sought by the PNSR and various Members of Congress:

- Formulate and enact annual foreign relations authorization bills;
- Provide greater flexibility on reprogramming (intradepartmental) and transfer (interdepartmental) of funds for multiagency activities;
- Consolidate oversight of the DHS to one authorizing committee and one appropriations subcommittee per chamber;
- Create a common set of financial and other forms required of nominees for use by the White House and Senate;
- End the practice of honoring a hold by one or more Senators on a nominee for a position in a national security department or agency;
- Require that each nomination for one of the 10 most senior positions in a national security department or agency would be placed on the executive calendar of the Senate with or without a committee recommendation after 30 days of legislative session; and,
- Establish the expectation that each presidential appointee—unless disabled, experiencing a hardship, requested to resign by the President,

or appointed to another government position—
would serve until the President has appointed
his or her successor.

ENDNOTES - CHAPTER 5

1. Project on National Security Reform (PNSR), *Forging a New Shield*, Arlington, VA: PNSR, November 2008.

2. Project on National Security Reform, *Toward Integrating Complex International Missions: Lessons from the National Counterterrorism Center's Directorate of Strategic Operational Planning*, Arlington, VA: PNSR, February 2010, available from *www.pnsr.org/data/files/pnsr_nctc_dsop_report.pdf*.

3. Project on National Security Reform, *Turning Ideas into Action*, Arlington, VA: PNSR, 2008, available from *www.pnsr.org/data/files/pnsr_turning_ideas_into_action.pdf*.

4. *Forging a New Shield*, p. 352.

5. See 50 USC § 404a. The Goldwater-Nichols Act of 1986 mandated an annual transmission by the executive branch of a national security strategy report to Congress within 150 days after an administration takes office. This mandate is not always met, and the National Security Strategy (NSS) document is a public, usually rhetorical, document, rather than one that provides a practical context for the national security system to make strategic decisions. An amendment to make the National Security Strategy a quadrennial requirement due 365 days after an administration takes office with updates as needed would allow more time for thoughtful policy input and make the NSS's production align more with actual practice.

6. "2010 QDR Terms of Reference Fact Sheet," Washington, DC: Department of Defense, April 17, 2009, available from *www.defenselink.mil/news/d20090429qdr.pdf*.

7. United States. Cong. House. H.R. 2410, *Foreign Relations Authorization Act, Fiscal Years 2010 and 2011*, introduced in the U.S. House; May 14, 2009, 111th Cong., 1st Sess., Washington: U.S. Government Printing Office (GPO), 2009, available from *http://www.govtrack.us/congress/billtext.xpd?bill=h111-2410*.

8. *Ibid.*

9. United States. Cong. House. H.R. 4974, *Quadrennial National Security Review Act,* introduced in the U.S. House of Representatives; March 25, 2010, 111th Cong., 2nd Sess., available from *http://www.govtrack.us/congress/billtext.xpd?bill=h111-4974.*

10. *Forging a New Shield*, pp. 340-351.

11. *Ibid.,* p. 130. See also Michael Leonard, "Matching Policy and Strategy with Resources," PNSR Issue Brief, August 10, 2009, available from *www.pnsr.org/data/files/matching%20policy%20 and%20strategy%20with%20resources-%20web%20brief.pdf.*

12. *Recalibrating the System: Toward Efficient and Effective Resourcing of National Preparedness,* Arlington, VA: PNSR, December 2009, available from *www.pnsr.org/data/files/pnsr_national_preparedness_system.pdf.*

13. *Forging a New Shield,* p. 260.

14. Civilian Personnel Management Service, "Defense Senior Leader Development Program, (DSLDP): Informational Briefing," Washington, DC: Department of Defense, June 2009, September 2, 2009, available from *www.cpms.osd.mil/ASSETS/ BD3F17FE13824136B1FDF34CBEA1B751/DSLDP%20Program%20 Brief%20v%20%20June%20w%2009%206-8-09%20chgs.pdf.*

15. For example, see the human capital management-related Intelligence Community Directives (ICD) 601, 610, 650, 651, 652, 653, 654, 655, 656, September 20, 2009, available from *www.dni. gov/electronic_reading_room.htm.*

16. The Markle Foundation Task Force on National Security in the Information Age, *Nation at Risk: Policy Makers Need Better Information to Protect the Country,* New York: The Markle Foundation, March 1, 2009.

17. *The United States Commission on National Security/21st Century (The Hart-Rudman Commission) Phase III Report,* "Road Map for National Security: Imperative for Change," March 15, 2001, p. 111.

18. National Commission on Terrorist Attacks Upon the United States, *The 9/11 Commission Report*, New York: Norton, 2004, p. 420.

19. *Beyond Goldwater-Nichols: U.S. Government and Defense Reform for a New Strategic Era, Phase I Report*, Washington, DC: Center for Strategic and International Studies, March 2004, p. 68.

20. Joel D. Aberbach, *Keeping a Watchful Eye: The Politics of Congressional Oversight*, Washington, DC: The Brookings Institution, 1990, p. 187 .

21. U.S. Senate Committee on Foreign Relations, "Jurisdiction of the Committee on Foreign Relations, United States Senate (Excerpted from Rules of the Committee), "Membership and Jurisdiction of Subcommittees of The Committee on Foreign Relations," September 2009, available from *webcache.googleusercontent. com/search?q=cache:pybFu8sLxtoJ:foreign.senate.gov/about/jurisdictio n/+study+and+review+on+a+comprehensive+basis,+matters+relating +to+the+national+security+policy,+foreign+policy,+and+internationa l+economic+policy+as+it+relates+to+the+foreign+policy+of+the+Un ited+States&cd=1&hl=en&ct=clnk&gl=us&source=www.google.com.*

CHAPTER 6

THE NATIONAL SECURITY COUNCIL SYSTEM: IT'S NOT MUCH, BUT WE LIKE IT

Harvey Sicherman

INTRODUCTION

Memoirs of the American national security system often read as if they were a new installment of the Pinocchio story, so often do noses grow and fingers point, especially during interagency meetings. Policymaking through this system sometimes appears to be an unnatural act, unnatural being defined by where one sits in a convoluted process established in 1947 and periodically updated, though not necessarily for the better. These pathologies are well known, and always reflect a want of executive leadership. Presidents who demean the system should not expect much of it, and a White House bereft of broad policy ideas will always be a victim of parochial departmental pursuits. That said, both enduring themes of national security reform and President Barack Obama's changes to the National Security Council (NSC) system are best understood in historic context. That perspective suggests two major points.

First, patterns do exist; namely, a pair of very different approaches emerging from the 1947 National Security Act, each with virtues and vices. These may be called the Truman-Acheson model (1948-52) on the one side, and the early Nixon-Kissinger model (1969-70) as its opposite. I shall also discuss each model's dysfunctional version, Reagan-Haig (1981-82) and the later Nixon-Kissinger (1971-72, before the latter became Secretary of State). This chapter will also cover the most recent and effective of these models—the Bush-Scowcroft-Baker system (1989-92).

Second, the Obama administration appears to be a hybrid in this context, one intended to be like that of President George H. W. Bush but overly centered in the White House. For several reasons it will not wear well. Still, in the final analysis, those who would try to transform the system should understand that it endures because presidents who understand it, like it.

"PRESENT AT THE CREATION": THE TRUMAN-ACHESON MODEL

Timing suggests that the NSC system, dating as it does from 1947, was conceived as a device with which to fight the Cold War. But the evidence argues for a less flattering origin, reflecting the tendency of governments to back firmly into the future. Those who invented it had World War II and Franklin Roosevelt in mind, not Harry Truman or the incipient U.S.-Soviet rivalry.

By 1946, the United States had emerged as the mightiest democracy. Its resources, its influence, and the consequences of its policies were now of global strategic significance. The aftermath of World War II meant that America's traditional policies, including diplomatic isolation and a very small standing army among others, were no longer up to the task of securing the United States. How then, the question is, to create an executive branch up to the challenge?

Those who promoted a new national security system were all men steeped in the immediate experience of mobilizing a nation for a two-front war. They had been mightily impressed by Winston Churchill's handling machine, the Imperial General Staff, and cut their teeth on the Allied Joint Staff. These seemed to work: The President was well served by an organization that gave him critical information, competing views, and efficient execution. But military policy was not the whole of national security.

The overall picture was decidedly different. President Franklin Roosevelt (FDR), who once described himself as a "juggler," dealt with a floating cast of characters, overlapping missions, and secretive assignments.[1] He evinced little respect for Cabinet departments or his own appointees. FDR's crucial first visit with Winston Churchill off Newfoundland in 1941, for example, was concealed from his Secretary of State and his Secretary of War, neither of whom attended.

The new system embodied in the 1947 National Security Act therefore was intended to give the President a permanent organization to coordinate action while simultaneously establishing order in the relations between the Cabinet and the President. Its birth, however, was assisted by numerous midwives, some of whom had different expectations of the infant. Its upbringing and education predictably became controversial. The new U.S. Secretary of Defense, James Forrestal, believed that a civilian version of the Joint Staff would rely on Department of Defense (DoD) personnel rather than on White House appointees. He was wrong. The U.S. Secretary of State, General George Marshall, feared for the State Department's primacy in a council that might be dominated by other departments. He was right.[2]

Truman himself seemed to have grasped the inherent difficulties in the twin objectives of more presidential control, yet greater presidential accountability. He fully supported the need for an orderly system, which, to use James Locher's felicitous phrase, "occupies that space between the departments and the president."[3] The man from Missouri had himself been a victim of FDR's methods, entering the presidency upon Roosevelt's sudden death completely unaware of his predecessor's international arrangements. That said, he was also acutely aware of the challenges to his authority from both the political opposition and FDR loyalists who deemed him unworthy. These circumstances made him more, rather than less, eager to show that the buck stopped on his desk. So, as he took pains to point out in his memoirs, "I used the National Security Council only as a place for recommendations to be worked out."[4] Like the Cabinet, the Council does not make decisions. The policy itself has to come down from the President, as all final decisions have to be made by him.[5] President Truman was accountable to Congress and the American people, and bound by the Constitution. He was not accountable to the NSC.

That being so, at least one premise of the new system was questionable. It might very well suit the style of someone like Truman, who, although he was a strong partisan of his own prerogative, also favored Cabinet responsibility. His appointees were his staff, and the NSC eventually became for him a good forum to exercise orderly government. But what of a President who wanted to run part or all of national security policy from the White House? Or a latter-day juggler, like FDR? Or simply a chief executive who wanted decisions made in another forum? This might render the NSC system useless, or confusing at best. As we shall see, that is precisely what happened.

The Truman administration's NSC functioned without an advisor, and the President's assistant simply acted as an administrator. In its early years, Truman did not view NSC meetings as compelling, attending only 12 of 57 before the Korean War. The Act was amended in 1949 to make the NSC more useful. Still, it would be wrong to describe the set-up as weak; its test was whether it helped the President to decide and execute. Truman, although keen on his prerogatives, believed in Cabinet government, not total control from the White House. The entire system benefited from the surprising relationship between a very odd couple, Truman and his Secretary of State, Dean Acheson. This accidental President — Midwestern, lower middle class, and largely self-educated in history — got along famously with the imperious, superbly cultivated, and worldly establishment lawyer. Their mutual confidence was reflected in a telling bureaucratic detail; Acheson chaired NSC meetings in Truman's absence, a sure sign of State's preeminence.

Years later, Acheson succinctly summarized the Truman era's achievement, "to create half a world, a free half, out of the same material without blowing the whole to pieces in the process."[6] How much did the NSC contribute? It is important here to distinguish between process and result. One can have an orderly process, yet one that will not guarantee the correct decision. The record amply illustrates the point.

Truman's team produced two of the great strategic documents of American history. George Kennan's long telegram (1946) and subsequent X article in *Foreign Affairs* stood the test of long-term analysis, laying the basis for the so-called "containment strategy." Kennan's work, of course, preceded the NSC's formation. But the strategy that embodied his insights was the product of the NSC. Its staff, ably led by Acheson's Policy Planning chief, Paul Nitze, undertook the production of what became NSC-68 as part of the decision to build the H-Bomb. Here was the new system doing what it was designed to do: bringing together disparate dimensions of the problem and relating means to ends. Acheson saw the study as a way to fill the widening gap between U.S. conventional capabilities and its new international commitments.

By all accounts, too, the NSC performed its crisis management task during the Korean War. Truman's personal attendance at 64 of the 71 meetings between June 1950 and the end of his term testified to its utility as a wartime tool. Thus, despite its early sketchy performance, by the end of the Truman administration, the NSC tool in the context of a strong President-Cabinet team had proven its utility as both long-range planner and crisis manager.[7]

Still, as noted earlier, an effective process does not necessarily guarantee results. NSC-68, however fruitful its long-term yield, came too late to save Truman and the United States from the consequences of that military gap when North Korea invaded the South in June 1950, only 4 weeks after the completion of the document and before its cost could be fully calculated. Nor did it spare the President from authorizing General Douglas MacArthur's offensive that brought China into the war, possibly the product of what the late Peter Rodman called "too much collegiality around the National Security Council table."[8] Even Acheson, experienced and combative as he was, noted ruefully that no one had quite crystallized the potential worst case, thereby letting Truman down. The Secretary of State thus acknowledged that the ever-present pressure to agree with a President once he indicates his preferences was still at play, the NSC structure notwithstanding.

REAGAN-HAIG: "THE GHOST SHIP"

The dangers of trying to fix on a president a national security system at odds with his personal predilections is well-illustrated by the Reagan-Haig experience (1981-82). On the surface it began as a duplicate of Truman-Acheson, but Reagan was not Truman, and therefore Haig could not be Acheson.

Unlike Truman, Ronald Reagan became President on the strength of a huge electoral victory. An older man schooled in the ways of the Midwest and Hollywood of an earlier era, Reagan had a gift for expressing American values. His purpose, as much domestic as foreign, was to restore American self-confidence and the winning ways of democracy and free enterprise.

Reagan had little foreign policy experience, but he harbored a few immutable convictions. He believed that the Soviet Union and communism were destined to fail of their own internal absurdities; that the United States and its allies had to firmly oppose Soviet attempts to enlarge their influence, especially through force; and that the proper mobilization of American moral and military power could achieve these ends without war, especially nuclear war. Putting these convictions into policy, however, required experts. General (Ret.) Alexander M. Haig, Jr. was to be Reagan's expert on foreign policy.

Haig had already served in the national security system at all levels, from a soldier in Korea to Supreme Commander of the Northern Atlantic Treaty Organization (NATO), from an assistant to Cyrus Vance in Lyndon Johnson's DoD under Robert McNamara, to Henry Kissinger's aide at the NSC. He functioned successfully as White House Chief of Staff during the Watergate crisis. Thus, Haig was the most experienced of his generation in what worked and did not work in the NSC system.

At first, Haig believed he had found in Reagan a strong believer in Cabinet government, similar to Truman. He secured from the President-elect authority to take the lead in foreign policy (be the "vicar"). Encouraged by Reagan's desire not to suffer rows between the NSC advisor, a downgraded post, and the Cabinet, he set about designing a system around State's primacy certainly in the spirit of Truman-Acheson.

Reagan's idea of Cabinet government, however, soon proved incompatible with Haig's. More than most presidents, he wanted consensus from his Cabinet, especially on issues where he lacked knowledge or convictions. He depended entirely on an inner circle of three assistants to achieve consensus, or, failing that, to spare him a decision that would appear to favor one Cabinet secretary over another.

Haig discovered this abruptly when he noticed the three aides sitting at the Cabinet table rather than on the side, their place in previous administrations.[9] His NSC memo setting up various committees was never signed, while, quite contrary to staff capabilities, the Vice-President, George H. W. Bush, whose advisors suspected Haig's presidential ambitions, became chairman of the crisis group. Sniping among State, Defense, and the White House provided happy hunting grounds for the media.

This dysfunctional system claimed Haig 18 months later amid the storms of the Falklands War and Israel's invasion of Lebanon. It threw off a shower of misleading signals, policies at cross purposes, and costly errors.[10] Haig's sheer persistence, however, saved both the U.S.-China relationship and the Egyptian-Israeli peace treaty, and where Reagan actually had a strong personal view, such as in U.S.-Soviet relations, Haig found the going much easier.

The "ghost ship" as Haig called it, where no one could be sure of the captain's preferences, suited Reagan's decisionmaking style, but it left the NSC system rudderless, uncertain of the White House's direction. Haig's replacement in July 1982 by George Shultz soon proved that the problem was not one of personalities. For the remainder of Reagan's presidency, Shultz often found his way blocked by U.S. Secretary of Defense Caspar Weinberger, with no one to resolve the resulting paralysis. The NSC advisors paid the personal price: Reagan had six in 8 years. Finally, in the wake of the NSC-centered Iran-Contra crisis, the Tower Commission Report identified the system itself as a contributing cause.[11]

The Reagan years were therefore an object lesson that presidents get the systems they want and the systems they deserve. On paper, Reagan-Haig and Reagan-Shultz looked like Truman-Acheson, but, in fact, Reagan's desire for consensus and his reliance on his immediate staff drained the formal process of its functions. In doing so, U.S. foreign policy, generally rated successful in fulfilling Reagan's objectives with respect to the Soviet Union, also suffered serious reverses in Central America and the Middle East that could be attributed, at least in part, to a malfunctioning system.

CONSENSUS AND CONFRONTATION: THE NIXON-KISSINGER MODEL

The Nixon-Kissinger model offers another conception of how the national security system should work as an instrument of presidential power. As we have seen already in the Truman-Acheson and Reagan-

Haig experiences, conceptions, personalities, and political circumstances shape operations regardless of formal structures.

Richard Nixon's election to the presidency in 1968 capped a long and controversial political career marked by dramatic ascents and descents. President Eisenhower's Vice-President, Nixon, barely lost to John Kennedy in 1960; his political career appeared over when he lost the California gubernatorial race years later. A man of the West Coast, he then moved to New York, but never lost his dislike of the Eastern establishment. After enormous efforts, 6 years later he barely won the presidency over Hubert Humphrey.

Nixon's America was convulsed by the Vietnam War, accompanied by social and economic upheaval. The new President was not a unifying figure. Widely reviled as "Tricky Dick" and an unregenerate Cold Warrior, he was by nature a shy man given to awkward gestures and deep suspicions. Yet there existed another Nixon, carefully self-tutored in foreign policy and passionately interested in history. You needed a President for foreign affairs, he would say, because a competent Cabinet could run the country.

Nixon was intimately familiar with Eisenhower's staff concept for the NSC and understood how the former general had used it to develop alternatives that allowed him nonetheless to move in his preferred direction. Nixon did not want the hidden-hand presidency though. He believed that to succeed, a President had to choose priorities and then pursue them relentlessly.

Nixon's Secretary of State, William Rogers, was an old friend from the Eisenhower and law practice days. To him would be subcontracted the foreign policy issues other than Nixon's top list: Vietnam, U.S.-Soviet relations, and China. Taking his political rival Nelson

Rockefeller's foreign policy advisor, Harvard Professor Henry Kissinger, as his NSC Advisor, Nixon would use the NSC not only to coordinate national security policy but to actually carry it out.

Much ink has been spilled on the psychology of the Nixon-Kissinger duo. Suffice to say, Nixon regarded the foreign policy establishment with the same suspicion he reserved for the elite in general; they would thwart him if they could. Kissinger, the refugee turned academic superstar, did not need tutoring in the politics of envious rivalry.

Thus, the new model was founded in part on presidential mistrust of the departments. Unlike Cabinet government with the NSC as coordinator, the President would use it partly in place of the Cabinet on several key issues. Kissinger and select members of his staff, including his able military assistant, Colonel Alexander M. Haig Jr., became the key executors of the policy itself. This operation notched several significant if very controversial achievements in a very short time: the strategy of Vietnamization; U.S.-Soviet détente; and above all, the opening to China.[12]

By the end of Nixon's first term, however, the model had begun to morph into something else. The bureaucracy, deeply affronted at its exclusion from key issues, fulfilled Nixon's expectations of resistance and sabotage. Worse, the State Department, in the President's eyes, mishandled parts of its subcontract, notably the Middle East, thereby threatening U.S.-Soviet relations in the process. Soon there were mixed signals about who was in charge of what. The Kissinger-Rogers rivalry set a sensational example (nearly duplicated by the Brzezinski-Vance combat in the Carter administration) upon which the media feasted.

Peter Rodman, who, as Kissinger's assistant, lived to tell the tale, described the extent to which the administration was a house divided against itself, keeping two or three sets of books on China, for example, (one for State, one for the DoD, and the real one); absurdly, a naval ensign turned out to be literally a spy for the DoD.[13] This was a system, or lack thereof, headed for a great fall until the lack of coordination was resolved by a single stroke: Henry Kissinger became Secretary of State in 1973.

Kissinger would serve as both National Security Advisor and Secretary of State for 1 1/2 years, coordinating the government's national security policy while restoring State's leadership in his own person. To State's surprise, he proved respectful of the Foreign Service, its skill and prerogatives. Writing about it years later, he would declare that the first negotiation facing a Secretary of State was that between the secretary and the Foreign Service. Upon its success depended all others.[14]

In sum, the Nixon-Kissinger model gave the President more direct and secretive operational control of key issues at the expense of the Cabinet departments. It could function well as long as boundaries were respected and subcontracts executed well. Under the pressure of events, however, it degenerated into expanding White House execution of policy and internecine warfare. Ironically, the Nixon-Kissinger model would be rescued in 1973 by a revival of the Truman model when Kissinger became U.S. Secretary of State.

BUSH-BAKER-SCOWCROFT: SYSTEMIC INTEGRITY

Having reviewed the contrasting models (Truman-Acheson; early Nixon-Kissinger) and examples of how each could become imbalanced (Reagan-Haig; late Nixon-Kissinger), one further example should be discussed. This was the very effective system run by President George H. W. Bush, Secretary of State James Baker III, and General Brent Scowcroft, Bush's National Security Advisor. It proved crucial in managing two unforeseen crises, namely, the end of the Cold War and Saddam Hussein's seizure of Kuwait.

Bush won the 1988 election decisively, but the new President did not regard his term as a mere extension of Reagan's. Part New England patrician and part Texas oil wild-catter, he was a veteran Washington insider with a special interest in foreign policy. Bush had served as Ambassador to the United Nations (UN) from 1971-73, de facto ambassador to China, and director of the Central Intelligence Agency (CIA). Not much for what he called derisively "the vision thing," he was an awkward public speaker and more a pragmatic administrator.

General Scowcroft, for his part, was also a consummate insider. He had worked on the civilian side of the government for some time. Scowcroft played a part at the NSC as early as 1955; he served as NSC deputy when Kissinger was both Secretary of State and NSC Advisor. He was then the Advisor from 1975 to 1976.

Finally, Bush selected as his Secretary of State his long-time confidante, James A. Baker III. An authentic Texan given to salty speech and agricultural metaphors, Baker was a sophisticated lawyer and political operative. He had been one of Reagan's three vital staff aides, escaping the crash of that arrangement by becoming Secretary of the Treasury in Reagan's second term. Unlike Bush or Scowcroft, he knew little of foreign policy, but had acquired considerable international experience through the negotiations over currency and trade agreements.

Bush, Scowcroft, and Baker had all been appalled in the Reagan years by what they saw as a dangerously defective NSC. Scowcroft himself had been co-author of the Tower Commission Report, which laid out the system's malfunctions. While the new President's own fascination with the subject and pragmatic bent meant that he would be hands on, this did not mean White House execution of foreign policy. As both Bush and Scowcroft recalled, they wanted a real workhorse at State who could conceive and execute policy at the President's direction.[15] There should be departmental or Cabinet responsibility, not a cabal of aides. Above all, there should be an orderly process that gave the national security establishment a role and a stake. Baker, supremely confident in his relationship with Bush, accepted these arrangements. He would make up for his lack of knowledge by employing the best people he could find and concentrating them on State's Policy Planning staff.

The three pragmatists did bring a few ideas with them. On the procedural level, Scowcroft wanted to revive the professional element in making policy; so one of the new administration's first acts was to call for an interagency review and assessment of policy. He also gave the NSC committees their 3-level form: principals, deputies, and policy coordinating committees.[16] As for policy itself, they wanted to substantiate much of the late Reagan-Gorbachev frothy rhetoric with real agreements to decrease tensions. The Cold

War was not nearly as much over as many believed; a dose of serious management would either ratchet it down or expose Mikhail Gorbachev as merely a clever propagandist. In any event, little change was expected in the basic European security architecture, locked in its NATO-Warsaw Pact dimensions.

Finally, while expectations on U.S.-Soviet relations were rather muted, the new administration had high hopes for dramatic change in Asia. Much of this derived from Bush's own analysis of China and Baker's international economic experience with the leading powers of the region, including a Japan then regarded as America's most serious commercial competitor.

All of these approaches were rapidly overcome by events. The interagency review cost the new administration time, resources, and initiative without producing any notable policy insights. Baker, a quick learner, later wrote, "In the end, what we received was mush."[17] By early spring, Bush had to work hard to counteract Gorbachev's "common European home" idea, settling on the State Department's phrase, "a Europe whole and free."[18] Then, in early June, the Tiananmen Square massacre ended hopes for much advance in U.S.-China relations. Last, and above all, Europe was transformed as the Berlin Wall fell and Germany was reunited.

Bush, Scowcroft, and Baker had expected to manage rather than innovate. Now they were faced with transformative events. The NSC system had to develop new strategic geopolitical concepts on the spot, but, as Scowcroft would later say, "That was one of the most frustrating things to me. Nobody else is in a position to do the broad, long-range thinking that the NSC is, but I don't know how you do it."[19] Thus, in a way remarkably similar to the Truman-Acheson period, policy planning at the State Department would develop the administration's overall strategy, filling the NSC vacuum.

This is not the place to relate every detail in a complex policy, the outcome of which was the peaceful reunification of Germany in NATO, a signal triumph for the United States.[20] For our purposes, one critical event will suffice: the process whereby the two-plus-four negotiating framework became American policy. This framework, agreed to by the Union of Soviet Socialist Republics (USSR), Britain, and France in early 1990, convened the four occupying powers of 1945 for a singular purpose--to facilitate the merger of the German Democratic Republic (GDR, or East Germany) with the Federal Republic of Germany (FRG, or West Germany).

The opening of the Berlin Wall on November 9, 1989, had been the most sensational of the tumultuous political events that replaced the Stalinist East German regime with what Gorbachev believed to be a stabilizing reformist government, but the situation did not settle down. East Germany's economy was rapidly deteriorating as workers went on strike, management and skilled people emigrated, and demonstrations continued. Gorbachev had a large army in East Germany, complete with dependents. Would he allow the GDR to slip into chaos, or would he attempt to save the state through military action? Both prospects carried the danger of violent and unpredictable consequences for the peace of Europe.

Beginning in mid-December, the author had raised with Dennis Ross, head of the Policy Planning staff, the four-power forum as the way out for Gorbachev between the choice of chaos or military action. To ease West German fears, the point of a four-power conference would be strictly defined, namely, to facilitate reunification of the Germanys. By definition then, the Soviets (plus the British and French) would already have conceded that the GDR would cease to exist, a huge advance in and of itself for Chancellor Helmut Kohl, who badly wanted a unified Germany firmly tied to NATO and the West. This was also President Bush's fundamental requirement.

The NSC staff, which included some notable Soviet and European experts, strongly opposed a revival of the four occupation powers as a vehicle to steady the situation. In their view, this would fatally damage U.S.-West German relations; the Kohl government, like its predecessors, regarded the idea that the 1945 victors would determine Germany's fate to be an intolerable affront to the sovereignty of the successful democracy that the Bonn republic had become. This view was strongly shared by the European Bureau at State. The alternative was to hope for a de facto reunification on the ground, which subsequent diplomacy might then ratify.[21]

By late January, however, Gorbachev had also come to realize that the GDR was slipping away, and he feared the existing alternatives. The message from Moscow was a call for assistance before matters got out of control. Paris, and especially London meanwhile, dreaded German unification.

Baker was persuaded by Policy Planning's proposal and secured Bush's approval to sound out German Foreign Minister Hans-Dietrich Genscher on what came to be called the two-plus-four framework. Genscher, a Free Democrat, was notably more eager to deal with Moscow than his Christian Democrat chief, Kohl. Bush, at Scowcroft's urging, had to check with Kohl at critical points in the diplomacy, a tricky maneuver for both leaders. Kohl proved very much in favor of his foreign minister's policy and the two-plus-four. For Bush, the matter was decided.

At this point, a badly run NSC operation would have opened a flood of leaks to the media intended by the opponents of the policy to drown it, especially when that opposition could draw on not only NSC staff professionals but also the European Bureau at State. It did not happen. General Scowcroft rallied his staff behind the policy and, indeed, imposed discipline on the rest of the national security bureaucracy. It worked. There were no mixed signals from Washington, and on February 12, 1990, the two-plus-four framework was agreed to at the Ottawa summit.

Curiously, the crucial transaction occurred on July 15-16, 1990, when Kohl and Gorbachev worked out essential military and financial details between them. The deal respected the basic two-plus-four parameters though a unified Germany in NATO, formally agreed to on September 12 in Moscow. Former Secretary of State George P. Shultz once lamented that presidential decisions were too often just a signal to begin a new stage of the same argument. In the case of German unification, however, Bush's decision on two-plus-four ended the argument, and Scowcroft enforced it — all the more impressive because his own experts and he himself disagreed with the policy. The peace and freedom of Europe were the beneficiaries.

Bush's NSC process was not always so skillful. The run-up to war in Kuwait, the other great surprise, found the administration struggling with its rationale for war. It was also plagued by DoD leaks about the dangers of military action. On other issues, such as the Balkans, the administration had already lost some of its grip as the 1992 election approached. State's ideas on Europe's future were put aside. Bush's, Scow-croft's, and Baker's last great achievement proved to be the Arab-Israeli peace conference, held in Madrid (October 1991) following Saddam's defeat.

The Bush-Baker-Scowcroft example reminds us that fundamental to a successful national security system is what may be called the integrity of the process. It consists of four vital and interlinked components:

1. The process matters: The interagency discussions contribute to final decisions without there being any end runs or secret channels. This encourages the participants to do their best.

2. The process is fair: Alternatives are heard, and the relevant departments contribute. There is no need to leak.

3. Talent is concentrated: The President can call upon a concentration of conceptual or strategic thinkers (at the NSC or, as was the case, in State's Policy Planning), not only tacticians.

4. Decisions are executed: Once decisions are made, the relevant departments carry them out.

ASSESSING OBAMA: A HYBRID SYSTEM

The two Presidents who followed George H. W. Bush did not give the NSC system its finest hours. Bill Clinton's verbose meetings rarely yielded conclusions; his presidency, by all accounts, was not orderly, and the NSC operation reflected as much. Moreover, in some respects, the staff became operational rather than primarily analytical, especially in the counterterrorism area.[22]

By contrast, George W. Bush's NSC was intended as a reversion to the Scowcroft model. Directed by Condoleezza Rice, a veteran of the 1989-90 experience,

the NSC staff became primarily analytical.[23]   After
September 11, 2001 (9/11), however, all of these intentions were subsumed into crisis management. The
DoD and the White House, notably the Vice President,
overshadowed State. In the eyes of the critics, the NSC
system did not supply either an orderly process, a full
venting of different views, or a forum for decisionmaking. Only in Bush's second term, when Rice became Secretary of State and her deputy, Stephen Had-
ley, succeeded her at the NSC, did the Council regain
its balance. Bush's decision in early 2007 to reverse
Iraq strategy in favor of a surge under the command
of General David Petraeus, DoD's arch counterinsurgency advocate, was the most significant outcome of
the new operation.

Under the impetus of these events, both the 9/11
Commission and what became a full-blown national
security reform movement advocated large-scale
changes.[24] The intent was to improve the NSC system's
coordinating and analytical functions, especially in
the face of a rapidly changing post-Cold War picture
in which economics played an increasingly important
role. Thus, when Barack Obama became President after a campaign promising change, the stage seemed
set for a different approach.

The new President was a political dramatist of the
first order. Unknown but a few years before, Barack
Obama parlayed a modest resume and unique biog-
raphy into a campaign that defeated decisively the
well-known and widely admired war hero, Senator
John McCain. This was all the more impressive, given
the continuing conflicts in Iraq and Afghanistan and a
sense of national alarm brought on by the severe economic crisis of September 2008.

Obama promised new ideas on foreign policy that would contrast with those of his predecessor. They proved sometimes to be different, but they were not new. Under the mantra of engagement, for example, the President emphasized the virtues of collective rather than unilateral or even allied action, a theme reminiscent of Jimmy Carter or Woodrow Wilson. As for the detailed policies, these were drawn largely from a consensus, often of a bipartisan nature. Thus, much of the new administration's Middle East activity could be found in the recommendations of the 2006 Baker-Hamilton Commission.[25] Obama's emphasis on a nuclear free world, to cite another example, drew on a bipartisan group headed by former Secretary of State Shultz.[26]

As for the national security system, Obama clearly had the Scowcroft precedent in mind. His NSC Advisor, Marine General James Jones, spoke of his role as coordinator and facilitator of the debates the President needed to hear. The three-level organization originated by Scrowcroft was retained.[27] Obama's choice of his Democratic Party rival, Hillary Clinton, to serve as Secretary of State also suggested a strong Cabinet model.

In actuality however, Obama-Clinton-Jones would not be like Bush-Baker-Scowcroft, or Truman-Acheson. While both Obama and Clinton delivered major foreign policy speeches in the spring and summer of 2009, and Obama adopted State's slogan about engagement, the White House circumscribed State's role.[28] This was done not simply through rhetoric but by the appointment of special representatives on critical issues, notably, former Senator George Mitchell in the Israeli-Palestinian conflict and Ambassador Richard Holbrooke for Afghanistan-Pakistan. Vice President

Joe Biden, an acknowledged foreign policy enthusiast throughout a long senatorial career, soon surfaced as a key figure in dealing with European, NATO, and Russian affairs when he was not busy with Iraq and Afghanistan. The signal sent abroad suggested that the special representatives, the Vice President, or the White House, were the primary addresses, not State.

State was not the only Cabinet department to be diminished; Homeland Security was another. On May 26, 2009, Obama combined the Homeland Security Council staff with the NSC under General Jones, but the Assistant to the President for Homeland Security and Counterterrorism, John Brennan, a CIA veteran, soon became the major administration spokesman.[29] This combined analytical/operational post resembled Richard Clarke's role in the last years of the Clinton administration, which was undone by Condoleezza Rice before 9/11.

The model, then, was very much a hybrid: an NSC advisor and the staff were to function like Scowcroft's with Cabinet personalities (including Secretary of Defense Robert Gates, a Bush holdover who, as deputy to Scowcroft and then CIA chief under George H. W. Bush, was intimately familiar with the Bush-Baker system); but, at least in the case of State and Homeland Security, functional control of several key issues was held by the White House itself—early Nixon.

How well is the hybrid working? Jones managed to do some streamlining in the name of coordination by incorporating the Homeland Security staff into the NSC. By his own account, he has tried to broaden the Council's analytical capability. Thus far, however, he has not touched the high-powered, and separate, national/economics council, nor is it clear whether these topics are a subject for NSC review.

The homeland security portion of these changes did not work very well. On December 25, 2009, a would-be suicide bomber bungled his mission on board an airplane bound for Detroit; he was subdued by passengers. After landing, he proved to be a Nigerian whose father had warned the State Department about his son's ways. This and other important elements did not sound an alarm for the National Counterterrorism Center. Worse yet, as U.S. Admiral Dennis C. Blair, then Director of National Intelligence, revealed, neither he (nor the NSC) had been consulted when the Justice Department decided to read the suspect his Miranda rights.[30] The coordination function had clearly failed in this case.

The system was also given a severe test on the Afghanistan issue. Here the analytical and coordinating role came under enormous pressure when the presidential preference for consensus required a reassessment. Obama had made Afghanistan his war. The President emphasized both the justness and significance of the effort to defeat al Qaeda, the main enemy of the redefined war on terrorism, or "violent extremism," to use the words of John Brennan, Obama's de facto czar on the subject.[31] In March 2010, Obama endorsed a strategy of counterterrorism in Afghanistan, approved troop reinforcement already underway, and also appointed a new commander, General Stanley McChrystal, to run the war.

Obama's course, however, had not been uncontested. Biden and others rejected the idea that what had worked in Iraq would work in Afghanistan. They favored a much more limited exercise that basically targeted al Qaeda. Their opposition surfaced when McChrystal, after assessing his strategic needs, reported through DoD that he needed another 40,000 troops.

Then Karzai was re-elected President in a corrupt August poll, throwing into question whether counter-insurgency could work with such a partner. Thereafter, the administration's low opinion and frequent upbraiding of the Afghan leader surfaced often, sometimes officially and sometimes through leaks.

On September 21, 2010, General McChrystal's dire estimate of the Afghan situation appeared in the newspapers. The leak prompted President Obama to remind the Joint Chiefs that he was commander in chief. Secretary of Defense Gates talked of the virtues of advice through the chain of command.[32]

His original consensus undone, President Obama called for a reassessment of the strategy. This was conducted through a vast number of meetings and reports under the coordination of the NSC.[33] Touted as a model exercise of its own, the reassessment went on for over 3 months. It, too, was disrupted by a serious leak, this time a cable from the U.S. Ambassador in Kabul, General Karl Eikenberrry, himself a one-time commander in Afghanistan under the earlier, discredited strategy. He argued vehemently against anything that counted on Karzai.[34] This leak effectively sundered relations with McChrystal, who had not been forewarned of Eikenberry's opinion; it also fatally damaged the ambassador's relations with Karzai. Nor was Special Representative Holbrooke on good terms with the Afghan leader. That left McChrystal as the only American official with a good working connection.

Finally, in late December, Obama announced his decision. He had cobbled together a fresh consensus. He would give McChrystal 30,000 more troops to pursue counterinsurgency. The strategy would be subject to major review a year later. July 2011 would mark the beginning of the U.S. withdrawal from Afghanistan, and responsibility would be shifted to the newly organized Afghan army and police units.

The latest compromise, like the earlier ones, put a greater premium on consensus at home than effectiveness in the field. It presumed a straight-line success almost on the Iraqi schedule and an Afghan government a whole lot more capable in a short time than anyone could imagine. All of this was undermined by the withdrawal date, itself clearly intended to hold the support of the Vice President and the many Democrats opposed to the strategy. Attempts by Petraeus, Clinton, and Gates to play down the significance of July 2011 were quickly countered by Biden, among others. These confusing signals could only have the most dire effect, as McChrystal struggled to persuade the Afghans that the surge was more than just a last effort to make things look better while actually simply being a cover for the end of the mission.

McChrystal himself became the victim of the December consensus, and by his own hand. The spring fighting, even with an abrupt and belated embrace of Karzai by Obama, did not go as well as planned. Once more the administration began to divide, and the leaks multiplied. Then, in the third week of June 2010, McChrystal and his staff were exposed by an about-to-be-published account of their disdain for the Obama team's management of the war.[35] On June 23, 2010, McChrystal resigned, to be replaced by the architect of the Iraqi surge and the Afghanistan strategy, General David Petraeus.

As the President pointed out, it was not a difference over strategy, but rather the way the general had complained through the media that compelled his departure. At the heart of McChrystal's complaints, though, was the disarray on the civilian side. Were Eikenberry and Biden, for example, really behind the strategy? Or had the December review and July 2011 date simply held them off? The President, the Secretary of State, the Chairman of the Joint Chiefs of Staff, and General Petraeus all hastened to explain that these mileposts were not cast in cement. Obama also chastised his team the day of McChrystal's resignation for petty quarrels that hurt the war effort. These repairs notwithstanding, Obama's method and his reliance on consensus had revealed that the resulting policy was either incoherent (the withdrawal date issue) or ineffective (mixed signals from too many officials). And the leaking suggested flaws in the NSC system's integrity, or, at the least, its discipline.

To sum up: Obama had combined something of the Bush-Baker model and something of the Nixon-Kissinger model but without the balances that would make the hybrid work. Unlike Bush-Baker, Clinton's State Department had a secondary role, and unlike Nixon-Kissinger, consensus politics robbed the White House's primacy of disciplined coherence. This is unlikely to last. The pressure of untoward events will push the system more toward one model or the other.

The way will thus be open once more to reform. Before we get too excited about such prospects, though, this article's historical perspective may be useful. Three points may be extracted from the record:

1. **Presidents must choose their paradigm**: Either Truman-Acheson; its lineal successor, Bush-Baker; or early Nixon-Kissinger will do, so long as its chief executive understands the consequences.

2. **Integrity is all**: The process cannot work well unless it is to be seen as important, inclusive, thoughtful, and decisive.

3. **Strategy counts**: The tendency of crisis management to cancel out strategy can only be counteracted by the creation of an effective "strategy cell" of people tasked to do it either at State's Policy Planning or in the NSC staff.

Last but not least, perhaps the final judgment on the NSC system as we have known it since 1947 may be found in a dialogue from the 1968 Clint Eastwood film, *Coogan's Bluff*. Eastwood plays a Western marshal sent to recover a fugitive under custody of the New York Police. After suitable smashing of the china, he is confronted dramatically by a surly New York detective played by Lee J. Cobb. Cobb tells Eastwood, "Now, we have a system here. It's not much, but we like it!"

Presidents have not always understood the national security system they inherit. Nor have they always used it to great effect, but like Harry Truman, Richard Nixon, or George H. W. Bush, once they did grasp its utility for the power of the presidency, they liked it. All would-be reformers should heed this experience; for, while the integrity of the system, as illustrated by the Bush-Baker-Scowcroft experience, is necessary for success, it is not sufficient. For that, reform must appeal, above all, to the President himself. Nothing less is likely to work.

ENDNOTES - CHAPTER 6

1. See Alfred D. Sander, "Truman and the National Security Council: 1945-1947," *Journal of American History*, Vol. 59, September 1972. This juggler reference comes from Secretary of the Treasury Henry M. Morgenthau, Jr.'s, diary, May 15, 1942. Referenced in Peter Rodman, *Presidential Command*, New York: Knopf, 2010, p. 296.

2. A short good recent account is found in Rodman, pp. 15-24.

3. James R. Locher III, "Leadership and the National Security Reform Agenda," Colloquium Report, Joseph R. Cerami, Robin Dorff, and Lisa M. Moorman, eds., *Leadership and National Security Reform: The Next President's Agenda*, Carlisle, PA: Strategic Studies Institute, U.S. Army War College, October 2008, p. 25, available from *www.strategicstudiesinstitute.army.mil/pdffiles/PUB888.pdf*.

4. Harry S. Truman, *Years of Trial and Hope*, Garden City, NY: Doubleday, 1956, p. 59.

5. *Ibid.*

6. Dean Acheson, "Apologia Pro Libre Hoc" in *Present at the Creation: My Years in the State Department*, New York: W. W. Norton & Co., 1969, p. xvii.

7. Although some scholars use Eisenhower's NSC as the "foundational model," from my perspective, Eisenhower simply filled in the planning and staff logic of the system he inherited, just as he provided the resources to flush out NSC 68's strategy; the real foundation for the NSC's function was laid under Truman. See, for example, John P. Burke, "The National Security Advisor and Staff: Transition Challenges," *Presidential Studies Quarterly*, Vol. 39, No. 2, June 2009.

8. Rodman, *Presidential Command*; Robert L. Beisner, *Dean Acheson: A Life in the Cold War*, New York: Oxford University Press, 2006.

9. Alexander M. Haig, Jr., *Caveat: Realism, Reagan and Foreign Policy*, New York: MacMillan, 1984, p. 80.

10. See my memorial essay, "Patriot: Alexander M. Haig, Jr.," *Orbis*, Vol. 54, No. 3, Summer 2010, pp. 344-345, 351-352.

11. John Tower, Edmund Muskie, and Brent Scowcroft, *The Tower Commission Report: The Full Text of the President's Special Review Board*, New York: Random House, 1987, pp. 62-63.

12. Rodman, p. 69.

13. *Ibid.*, pp. 66-67, especially p. 54.

14. Henry Kissinger, *Years of Upheaval,* Boston, MA: Little, Brown, 1982, p. 446.

15. George H. W. Bush and Brent Scowcroft, *A World Transformed,* New York: Alfred A. Knopf, 1998, p. 31.

16. Burke, "The National Security Advisor and Staff: Transition Challenges,"pp. 23-24. See also David Rothkopf, *Running the World*, New York: Public Affairs, 2005, pp. 266-67.

17. James A. Baker III, *The Politics of Diplomacy: Revolution, War, and Peace. 1989-1992,* New York: G P Putnam's Sons, 1995, p. 68.

18. Philip D. Zelikow and Condoleezza Rice, *Germany Unified and Europe Transformed: A Study in Statecraft*, Cambridge, MA: Harvard University Press, 1995, p. 31.

19. John P. Burke, *Honest Broker?: The National Security Advisor and Presidential Decision Making,* College Station, TX: Texas A&M University Press, 2009, pp. 173-174.

20. For a recent treatment, see Mary Elise Sarotte, *1989: The Struggle to Create Post-Cold War Europe,* Princeton, NJ: Princeton University Press, 2009.

21. Zelikow and Rice, p. 167.

22. Richard Clarke, *Against All Enemies: Inside America's War on Terror*, New York: The Free Press, 2004. See also Colin Powell and Joseph E. Persico, *My American Journey*, New York: Random House, 2003, pp. 547-550, 572-573, for an account of President Clinton's meetings.

23. Powell and Persico, *My American Journey;* Clarke, *Against All Enemies.*

24. 9-11 Commission. *The 9/11 Commission Report: Final Report of the National Commission on Terrorist Attacks upon the United*

States--Authorized Edition, New York: W. W. Norton & Company, July 22, 2004, paperback Ed., "PNSR Recommendations: Forging a New Shield," *Project on National Security Reform*, November 2008, available from *pnsr.org/data/files/pnsr%20forging%20a%20 new%20shield.pdf*; "Turning Ideas into Action," *Project on National Security Reform*, September 2009, available from *www.pnsr.org/ data/files/pnsr_turning_ideas_into_action.pdf*. A good review of the reform debate may be found in Catherine Dale, Nina M. Serafino, and Pat Towell, "CRS Report: Organizing the U.S. Government for National Security: Overview of the Interagency Reform Debates," Washington, DC: Congressional Research Service, December 2008.

25. *The Iraq Study Group Report*, James A. Baker, III, and Lee H. Hamilton, co-chairs; Lawrence S. Eagleburger *et al.*, New York: Vintage Books, 2006, available from *www.usip.org/isg/iraq_study_ group_report/report/1206/iraq_study_group_report.pdf*.

26. For more information, see the Nuclear Security Project, available from *nuclearsecurityproject.org*;

27. "Presidential Policy Directive–1: Organization of the National Security Council System," Washington, DC: The White House, February 13, 2009.

28. See my article, "Obama's Foreign Policy at Ten Months: the Limits of Consensus," *FPRI E-Notes*, November 2009.

29."A New Approach to Safeguarding Americans," Remarks by John O. Brennan, Assistant to the President for Homeland Security and Counterterrorism, prepared for delivery at the Center for Strategic and International Studies, August 6, 2009, Washington, DC, available from *www.whitehouse.gov/the_press_office/ Remarks-by-John-Brennan-at-the-Center-for-Strategic-and-International-Studies/*.

30. "REPORT 2010 111–199: Unclassified Executive Summary of the Committee Report on the Attempted Terrorist Attack on Northwest Airlines Flight 253," *Report of the Select Committee on Intelligence United States Senate*, May 24, 2010.

31. Brennan, "A New Approach to Safeguarding Americans."

32. "Remarks Delivered by Secretary of Defense Robert M. Gates," Washington, DC: Association of the United States Army, October 5, 2009, available from *www.defense.gov/speeches/speech.aspx?speechid=1383*

33. "Briefing by White House Press Secretary Robert Gibbs," Washington, DC: The White House: Office of the Press Secretary, October 30, 2009, available from *www.whitehouse.gov/the-press-office/briefing-white-house-press-secretary-robert-gibbs-103009.*

34. Greg Jaffe, Scott Wilson, and Karen DeYoung, "U.S. Envoy Resists Increase in Troops, Concerns Voiced About Karzai, Cables Sent as Obama Weighs Deployment Options," *The Washington Post*, November 12, 2009.

35. Michael Hastings, "The Runaway General," *Rolling Stone Magazine*, July 22, 2010.

CHAPTER 7

ASSESSING THE UNITED STATES IN AFGHANISTAN:
THE RECORD AND THE RANGE OF CHOICE

Joseph J. Collins

INTRODUCTION

U.S. efforts and prospects in Afghanistan stand at the intersection of five major vectors. These vectors are likely to foster change before and after July 2011 (7/11), the date when the President has said that "our troops will begin to come home."[1] Some conservatives in the West might prefer to fight on, shift later to a security assistance strategy, and deal with reconciliation and reintegration as a third priority. This may not be possible. Change in Afghanistan may not follow a linear pattern. While the United States should seek to shape events, it needs to be ready to react to changes that originate from events, contextual factors, or the actions of third parties. To understand why this is true, one must first understand the vectors that constitute the context for our future strategy, and then how those vectors developed over time.

U.S. objectives remain our guide and provide the first vector. Two successive U.S. Presidents have declared that the war in Afghanistan is a vital interest. Long after September 11, 2001 (9/11), the administration is still rightfully focused on the defeat or degradation of al Qaeda and its associated movements, one of which is the Afghan Taliban. Confounding those who doubted his will, President Barack Obama in the first 14 months of his administration has twice reinforced the U.S. contingent of now nearly 100,000 service members in Afghanistan; 45,000 Allied soldiers and 235,000 Afghan soldiers and police officers are also in the fight. In his first 14 months in office, according to the New America Foundation, President Obama has more than doubled the 2008 drone strikes (from 39 to 92 strikes) against terrorist targets in Afghanistan and Pakistan.[2] In a May visit to Washington, DC, Afghan President Karzai also received a promise from the Obama administration for a deeper, long-term strategic relationship that will cement the U.S.-Afghan partnership beyond the sound of the guns.[3] As the Iraq war fades, the "other war" in Afghanistan has become the main effort in the U.S. war on terrorism. It is impossible for any President to abandon or turn his or her back on such commitments.

Second, the costs of this war in time, blood, and treasure have been high. For the United States, the war has gone on for nearly 9 years, longer than U.S. combat troops were in Vietnam. For Afghanistan, the spring of 2010 marks 32 years of uninterrupted war. A thousand U.S. war dead, 750 fallen allies, and tens of thousands of Afghan dead bear silent witness to the high cost of this protracted conflict. June 2010, with more than 100 allied deaths, has been the worst month since the war started.[4] In a recent visit, General Kayani, the Pakistani Army Chief, reminded his U.S. audiences that in 2009 alone, the Pakistani Army suffered 10,000 casualties in its battles against the Pakistani Taliban.[5] Politically, most of the North Atlantic Treaty Organization (NATO) nations, including the United States, are wavering. In Europe, delicate coalition governments are dealing with serious fiscal problems and low public support for fighting in Afghanistan. American pleas for a larger European contribution have fallen on deaf ears, and most European combat contingents are likely to be withdrawn within a year. War weariness among all combatants will be a significant change agent in the next few years.

U.S. war expenditures in FY 2010 will likely exceed 80 billion dollars.[6] This enormous cost—on behalf of a country whose legal gross domestic product (GDP) is less than a third of that total—comes at a time of high unemployment and rampant deficit spending in the United States. As one wag told me: "We aren't yet at the bottom of our purse, but we can see it from here."[7] In the mid-term, budgetary constraints in the United States and Europe will begin to influence how the coalition pursues its objectives in Afghanistan.

Third, the enemy, generally successful from 2005 to 2009, is beginning to feel the heat of the Obama surge. Pakistan is slowly awakening to the danger of harboring violent extremist groups on its territory. Its soldiers have fought a war in the Northwest Frontier Province (renamed Khyber Paktoonkhwa) and South Waziristan to make that point. In Afghanistan, major allied offensives in the Pashtun-dominated south and east of Afghanistan highlight the Coalition's determination. In 2010 alone, U.S. Special Operations forces have killed or captured over 500 Taliban, over 100 of whom are senior Taliban officials.[8] U.S. Treasury experts on al Qaeda funding are turning their sharp eyes on the Taliban's financiers. One of the three major elements of the Afghan Taliban, Gulbuddin Hekmatyar's Hezb-i-Islami faction, has entered into direct talks with the Karzai government. Another part of the Taliban, the Haqqani network, with close InterServices Intelligence (ISI) and al Qaeda connections, has begun exploratory talks, using Pakistan as an intermediary. The Taliban is neither down nor out; it is still resilient and motivated, but for the first time it is feeling serious pressure from both its enemies and its benefactors.

Fourth, President Karzai's government remains weak, corrupt, ineffective, and by far, the Taliban's best talking point. The government that must win this war — if it is to be won — seems little more capable than it was in 2002. The Afghan government's police are a hindrance, its bureaucrats inefficient and corrupt, and its ministries ineffective. The narcotics industry may be a third the size of the entire legal economy. The effect of narcotics trafficking on both Taliban finances and Afghan governmental corruption is profound.

The level of governmental corruption was evident in the recent presidential election. Only the withdrawal of Karzai's most serious competitor, former foreign minister Abdullah Abdullah, enabled the current president to be legitimately called the winner. U.S. Ambassador Karl Eikenberry famously told U.S. Secretary of State Hillary Clinton and President Obama in November 2009 that Karzai "is not an adequate strategic partner."[9] More recent bickering had U.S. officials embarrassing Karzai by their public statements, while he bitterly denounced the United States and NATO for acting as occupiers, once even threatening to join the Taliban.

The May 2010 Karzai visit to Washington poured oil on these troubled waters, but it is not clear how long the calm seas will prevail. Friction within the U.S. team — the embassy, Holbrooke's team, and the military command — is evident. It is a key factor hobbling the U.S. ability to shape the situation in Afghanistan. Friction among decisionmakers was also a key factor underpinning General Stanley McChrystal and his staff's inappropriate and ill-timed remarks in *Rolling Stone*, which brought about his relief from command.[10]

In all, according to the United Nations (UN), despite much economic aid, Afghanistan, economically and socially, remains one of the bottom five countries in the world. There are, however, a few economic bright spots: Spurred by foreign aid, legal GDP growth has been robust; millions of Afghans use cell phones; indigenous radio and TV programs abound; and the Karzai government has increased revenue collection by 58 percent in the past year. Transportation, education, and health care have made marked improvements. The country has also begun to aggressively license the development of what may amount to 3 trillion dollars worth of mineral wealth.[11]

A final vector: After 32 years, the Afghan people are sick of war and tired of the intrusive presence of coalition forces. While International Security Assistance Force (ISAF)-involved civilian deaths and collateral damage are way down in the past year, growing Coalition forces are hard to live with. Fortunately, for the most part, the Afghan people despise the Taliban more than they dislike the government and its coalition partners. In national polls, the Taliban rarely rank higher than 10 percent. Most Afghans remember how repressive and ineffective the Taliban was at ruling their country from 1996 to 2001. With 40 nations helping the Karzai government today, the Afghan population also remembers that the Taliban regime was officially recognized by only three other countries. The vast majority of Pashtuns who live in the most violent areas, however, fear Taliban terror, and must sit on the fence for their own security.

The five vectors constitute the context for future strategic decisions in Afghanistan. The interaction of these variables has created a fluid environment where non-linear change is highly possible. The remainder of this chapter will cover what happened both on the battlefield and in stability operations that created the situation today, the decision to surge, and the way ahead.

WHAT HAPPENED, 2002-08?

There have been two phases in the war conducted under the banner of Operation ENDURING FREE-DOM. Despite the hoopla about the transformation of warfare and Green Berets on horseback calling in precision-guided bombs "danger close," the initial phase of Operation ENDURING FREEDOM was actually a conventional, albeit network-centric, military operation.[12] It featured Northern Alliance and anti-Taliban Pashtun ground forces (infantry and, in some places, cavalry) fighting a war of maneuver against the forces of the Taliban government and their legion of foreign supporters, many of whom were trained in al Qaeda camps in Afghanistan. The U.S. contribution came in the form of advice from U.S. Special Operations forces and Central Intelligence Agency (CIA) paramilitary personnel. The latter had provided yeoman service before 9/11 by maintaining close relations with Massoud and his Northern Alliance. These teams—approximately 600 people, in all—also connected friendly ground power to the awesome effects of American aircraft and unmanned aerial vehicles (UAVs). Former U.S. Secretary of Defense Donald Rumsfeld heralded the U.S. contribution and claimed that this operation was an example of defense transformation, but perhaps not the transformation that he intended:

> On the appointed day, one of their teams slipped in and hid well behind the lines, ready to call in airstrikes, and the bomb blasts would be the signal for

others to charge. When the moment came, they sig-
naled their targets to the coalition aircraft and looked
at their watches. Two minutes and 15 seconds, 10 seconds . . . and then, out of nowhere, precision-guided
bombs began to land on Taliban and al-Qaeda positions. The explosions were deafening, and the timing
so precise that, as the soldiers described it, hundreds
of Afghan horsemen literally came riding out of the
smoke, coming down on the enemy in clouds of dust
and flying shrapnel. A few carried RPGs. Some had as
little as 10 rounds for their weapons. And they rode
boldly . . . Americans, Afghans, towards the Taliban
and al Qaeda fighters. It was the first [horse] cavalry
attack of the 21st century . . . Now, what won the battle
for Mazar[-e-Sharif] and set in motion the Taliban's
fall from power was a combination of ingenuity of the
Special Forces, the most advanced precision-guided
munitions in the U.S. arsenal delivered by U.S. Navy,
Air Force and Marine crews, and the courage of the
Afghan fighters. . . . That day on the plains of Afghanistan, the 19th century met the 21st century, and they
defeated a dangerous and determined adversary, a
remarkable achievement.[13]

The initial campaign lasted from mid-October to
March 2002. The last operation, fraught with tactical
difficulties, broke up a hardcore Taliban and al Qaeda strongpoint in the Shahi Kot valley, northwest of
the Khost area. Overall, post-9/11 U.S. conventional
operations were impressive, and successful, but they
were not decisive. The United States neither destroyed
the enemy nor its will or ability to resist. The Taliban
field forces were defeated, and the regime ousted, but
much of the leadership of al Qaeda and the Taliban
escaped to safe havens in Pakistan and other nearby
countries.

The United States and its allies did not invite the
Taliban to participate in the Bonn Process to establish
a new government. In retrospect, this may have been

a mistake, but it was an understandable one. With help from the international community, Afghan leaders formed an interim government, without Taliban participation, with Hamid Karzai, a Durrani Pashtun of the Popalzai tribe, the traditional source of leaders in Afghanistan. The international community pledged over $5 billion in aid, and began the tough work of rebuilding a nation. After more than 2 decades of war, many believed that peace had come to the Hindu Kush.

The Taliban and al Qaeda, however, had other plans. They planned to hatch an insurgency to regain power in Kabul. Their hope was that the international community would tire of nation building under fire and would ultimately depart, leaving Karzai to the same horrible fate that befell Najibullah, the last communist ruler killed by the Taliban in the UN compound when they seized Kabul in 1996. The Taliban had sanctuaries in the Federally Administered Tribal Area (FATA) and Baluchistan in Pakistan, and other countries. They also quietly but obviously had strongpoints in a number of Afghan provinces, such as Helmand. Given the U.S. record, the insurgents felt that time was on their side. One familiar saying encapsulated their approach: The Americans have all the watches, but we have all the time.

Inside Afghanistan, Allied commanders and diplomats were astounded at the devastation that had been brought about by 23 years of war. The economy and society—rated by the UN in 1966 in the bottom five of all nation states —suffered mightily from 5 years of Taliban mismanagement and authoritarian rule, further complicated by a few years of drought. The country was only 30 percent literate, and 80 percent of its schools, neglected under the Taliban, had been destroyed in various wars. Of the Afghan children, 25 percent died before the age of 5. Only 9 percent of the population had access to health care. The professional and blue-collar work forces had virtually disappeared.[14]

Starting from the rock bottom in nearly every category, the government of Afghanistan and its coalition partners had a relatively easy time of it from 2002 to 2004. Progress was made in security, stabilization activities, and economic reconstruction. From 2003-05, the U.S. team, led by Ambassador Khalilzad and Lieutenant General Dave Barno, focused on teamwork and organization for Counterinsurgency (COIN) and stability operations. During this period of time, the relationship between Ambassador Khalilzad and President Karzai was very close and productive.[15] The government of Afghanistan, with much help from the international community, conducted nationwide *jirgas* (gatherings of community elders), passed a modern constitution, and held fair presidential and parliamentary elections in 2004 and 2005, respectively. These development efforts attracted a fair amount of international aid, but far less than the Balkan nations did after their conflicts in the 1990s.[16] U.S. security and economic assistance in these 3 years was a modest $4.4 billion, but nearly two-thirds of this went to economic assistance, with only slightly more that one-third to security assistance.[17] Using U.S. embassy statistics, the total foreign and security assistance (2002-08) per Afghan was approximately $270 per year.[18]

In the early years, under the guidance of Finance Minister Ashraf Ghani, the Afghan government swapped out the several viral currencies in use across the country, established a single stable currency, let international contracts for a nationwide cellular phone service, and began economic reconstruction. With the help of the international community, there was rapid reconstruction in health care and education. The ring road was rebuilt, furthering travel and commerce. Access to medical care was extended from less than 15 percent of the population under the Taliban to over 85 percent of Afghans.[19] Rapid economic growth began and has continued.

With the help of coalition forces and diplomats, the government's reach was tentatively extended to the provinces. Various countries, following the U.S. lead, set up Provincial Reconstruction Teams (PRTs) — small interagency elements to improve security and reconstruction — initially in a third of the provinces but now nearly nationwide. These 24 teams today play a key role in reconstruction and development.

The Afghanistan National Army (ANA) was brought into being, and an international peacekeeping force secured Kabul. More than 10,000 U.S. and allied forces conducted counterterrorism operations across the country. The U.S. Department of Defense (DoD) was wary at the start about talking about our efforts there as COIN. Some in the Bush administration were concerned specifically about limiting expectations for nation building, which was not a presidential priority in the first Bush administration. Progress was slow but steady, and the Taliban appeared to be relatively dormant. Kabul in particular, was calm as thousands of ISAF troops, mainly European, controlled security in the 225-mile area surrounding the capital.

The Taliban, however, was biding its time. From 2002 to 2005, the Taliban was rebuilding its cadres with drug money, so-called charity from donors in the Gulf states, and help from al Qaeda. Their sanctuaries in Baluchistan and the FATA enabled them to rearm, refit, and retrain. By 2005, the Quetta Shura Taliban, led by Mullah Omar; the Hezb-e-Islami Gulbuddin (HIG), led by Gulbuddin Hekmatyar; and the Haqqani Network, led by Jalaluddin Haqqani and his son, Sirajuddin, or Siraj, were all working together to subvert the Karzai regime, hoping to wear down the coalition. The Afghan government's lack of capacity and the allies' "light footprint" allowed many districts and a few provinces to remain under the quiet control of the Taliban.

In 2005, the Taliban began a nationwide offensive to spread its influence. From 2004 to 2009, there was a nine-fold increase in security incidents and a 40-fold increase in suicide bombing.[20] Conflict has spread to most of the 34 provinces, but 71 percent of the security incidents in 2010 have taken place in only 10 percent of the nearly 400 districts nationwide.[21] The war in Afghanistan today is still primarily a war over control of Pashtun areas in the eastern and southern portions of the country, but Taliban subversion and terrorism are important factors in many provinces across the country.

With lessons learned through al Qaeda in Iraq, the use of improvised explosive devices (IEDs) became the tactic of choice of the Taliban. IED strikes went from 300 in 2004 to more than 4,000 in 2009. Suicide bombers, almost unknown before 2004, became commonplace. By 2009 there were Taliban shadow governments in nearly all provinces. Even in areas dominated by the government or government-friendly tribes, Taliban subversion or terror tactics have become potent facts of life in many provinces.

Beginning in 2005, the Taliban added more sophisticated information operations and local subversion to their standard terrorist tactics. Sadly, those terror tac-

121

tics remained Standard Operating Procedures for the Taliban. In October 2008, for example, "the Taliban stopped a bus in the town of Maiwand, forcibly removed 50 passengers, and beheaded 30 of them."[22] A UN study in 2010, comparing 2009 to 2008, recorded a 14 percent increase in deaths totaling 2,412 personnel. Reflecting ISAF restraint, the report showed that the Taliban were responsible for the death of 70 percent of these Afghan civilians.[23]

How did the war in Afghanistan go from being a bright spot in the Global War on Terrorism (GWOT) to an issue in doubt? First, there was little progress in building Afghan governing capacity. To begin with, there was so little Afghan government and administrative capacity, that much economic and security assistance bypassed the Afghan government. Nations and international organizations found it more convenient to work through nongovernmental organizations (NGOs) and contractors. Over the years, the government in turn lost key ministers, like Ashraf Ghani, Abdullah Abdullah, and Ali Jalali, an early Minister of the Interior. There was much government corruption, often tied to police operations or the drug trade. Karzai was left alone by the Coalition to deal with the so-called warlords. Many of them ended up in the government. Others continued their viral existence in the provinces, often using their local power and business skills to rake off money from reconstruction projects or even from U.S. security contracts.

Second, Coalition arms, aid, trainers, and advisors ended up being too little, too slow, and too inefficient. U.S. and allied combat troops fared well, but the Coalition was unsuccessful in building up the capacity of the Afghan security forces, especially the police. Responsibility for police training was bounced from

Germany to the State Department to the DoD. Parts of that effort are still in transition. Army and police trainers and advisers are still in short supply. Being a weak link in the security chain, the Taliban has made attacking the police a priority. From 2007 to 2009, Afghan security forces killed in action (2,943) outnumber U.S. and allied dead (774) by a factor of nearly 4 to 1. More than two out of every three Afghan service members killed were policemen.[24]

In all, from 2004 to 2009, there were insufficient Coalition forces or Afghan national security forces to "clear, hold, and build." The Taliban had great latitude in picking their targets. Coalition military efforts often resembled the game of whack-a-mole, in which a sweep would go after the Taliban, who would go into hiding until the Coalition forces left. Taliban penetration of many areas deepened over time. Subversion, terrorism, and night letters from the local Taliban ruled many apparently safe districts by night.

It is not true that initial U.S. operations in Iraq stripped Afghanistan of what it needed to fight the Taliban. While some intelligence, surveillance and reconnaissaince (ISR) assets and Special Forces were removed from Afghanistan, most of the assets needed to continue the operation there were wisely fenced by Pentagon and Central Command (CENTCOM) planners.[25] It is fair to say, however, that post-2005, as the situation in Afghanistan began to decline, the much greater scope and intensity of problems in Iraq prevented reinforcements from being sent to Afghanistan. Perhaps more important, the near-desperate straits in Iraq up to mid-2007 kept U.S. leaders from focusing on fixing our efforts in Afghanistan. It was not until the obvious success of the surge in Iraq that U.S. decisionmakers were able to turn their attention to the increasingly dire situation in Afghanistan. With the advent of the Obama administration and improvements in Iraq, Afghanistan became the top priority in the War on Terrorism.

By the start of the Obama administration, security in Afghanistan was down, as was Afghan optimism about the future. Karzai's popularity declined, and confidence in the United States and its allies was halved. Many Afghans believed that the Taliban had grown stronger every year since 2005, and incentives for fence-sitting increased along with fear and disgust at government corruption. A new strategy was clearly needed.[26]

THE DECISION TO SURGE

The United States decided to surge in Afghanistan when it became feasible, but it took nearly a year to bring it to fruition. The foundation of the surge was laid by President George W. Bush in 2008, but the construction was completed under President Obama in 2009 and 2010. Studies on the U.S. strategy in Afghanistan began in the last year of the Bush administration. The most critical study of all was reportedly the one conducted under the auspices of the Bush National Security Council (NSC) staff.[27]

There was a preliminary decision to recommend to President Bush an increase in forces, but this was delayed to give the new team a chance to study the situation and make its own recommendations. Early on, President Obama, and his team conducted their own studies, which incorporated the work of the previous administration. Bruce Reidel of RAND supervised the efforts, which were facilitated by the continued presence on the NSC staff of U.S. Army Lieutenant General Doug Lute, who managed the war for the previous administration's NSC and has been an essential element in the continuity of our Afghanistan policy between the administrations.

In March, President Obama decided to alter the strategy. His 6-page March 27, 2009, White Paper contained the guts of a broad counterinsurgency program aimed at thwarting al Qaeda, "reversing the Taliban's momentum in Afghanistan," increasing aid to both Pakistan and Afghanistan, and forging a more united strategic approach to both countries.[28] In a parallel action, the President replaced the U.S. and ISAF commander, General David McKiernan, with General Stanley McChrystal, the then-Director of the Joint Staff and a highly experienced commander of Special Operations forces in both Iraq and Afghanistan. McChrystal was directed by the Secretary of Defense to conduct an assessment of our current efforts and report back to the White House. His August assessment was leaked to the press, and it was followed by a detailed in-house assessment and decisionmaking effort by President Obama over some 5 months.

President Obama's national security team examined various options. General McChrystal recommended a beefed-up, population-centric counterinsurgency strategy.[29] He identified two key threats: the insurgency and a crisis of confidence in the Karzai regime and the coalition. Key among his recommendations were greater partnering, increasing the size of the Afghan national security forces, improving governance, and gaining the initiative from the Taliban. He also recommended focusing resources on threatened populations, improving counternarcotics efforts, changing the culture of ISAF and adapting to restrictive rules of engagement to better protect the population. His initial assessment did not include a request for a troop increase, but he later requested a significant increase.

Other administration players had other ideas and they were debated for months with the active participation of the President. Some saw a need to focus more directly on al Qaeda; others wanted more emphasis on Pakistan. Yet, others wanted a delay because our Afghan allies had us balancing on a two-legged stool, while still others saw shifting priority to building the Afghan National Security Forces (ANSF, police and military) as the key to victory. Vice President Biden advocated a strategy focused on counterterrorism, without the expensive COIN and nation-building. As previously noted, Ambassador Karl Eikenberry, now on his third full tour in Afghanistan, was concerned with the inefficiency and corruption of the Karzai regime. He did not initially concur with U.S. reinforcements and recommended a shift of our top priority to preparing the ANSF to take over security and to work more closely with Pakistan.

President Obama outlined objectives in his West Point speech:

> We must deny al Qaeda a safe haven. We must reverse the Taliban momentum and deny it the ability to overthrow the government. And we must strengthen the capacity of Afghanistan's security forces and government so they can take lead responsibility for Afghanistan's future.[30]

To accomplish this, the President directed a surge of 30,000 U.S. troops, with the NATO allies adding nearly 10,000 to that total. To accompany this troop surge, the President ordered a surge of civilian officials, a great increase in foreign assistance, a decisive boost in funding for ANSF, increased aid to Pakistan, and support for Afghan reintegration and reconciliation efforts. The President also made it clear that the United States would not tolerate an open-ended commitment, an "endless war." The President directed that in July 2011 "our troops will begin to come home." He pointed out that the United States must balance all of its commitment. He rejected the notion that Afghanistan was another Vietnam. His message attempted to portray a firm national commitment, but not an indeterminate military commitment:

> There are those who acknowledge that we can't leave Afghanistan in its current state, but suggest that we go forward with the troops that we already have. But this would simply maintain a status quo in which we muddle through, and permit a slow deterioration of conditions there. It would ultimately prove more costly and prolong our stay in Afghanistan, because we would never be able to generate the conditions needed to train Afghan security forces and give them the space to take over.
>
> Finally, there are those who oppose identifying a time frame for our transition to Afghan responsibility. Indeed, some call for a more dramatic and open-ended escalation of our war effort . . . one that would commit us to a nation-building project of up to a decade. I reject this course because it sets goals that are beyond what can be achieved at a reasonable cost, and what we need to achieve to secure our interests. Furthermore, the absence of a time frame for transition would deny us any sense of urgency in working with the Afghan government. It must be clear that Afghans will have to take responsibility for their security, and that America has no interest in fighting an endless war in Afghanistan.

As President, I refuse to set goals that go beyond our responsibility, our means, or our interests. And I must weigh all of the challenges that our nation faces. I don't have the luxury of committing to just one. Indeed, I'm mindful of the words of President Eisenhower, who —-in discussing our national security —-said, 'Each proposal must be weighed in the light of a broader consideration: the need to maintain balance in and among national programs'.[31]

CONTENDING OPTIONS

In December 2010, the United States plans to take stock of its progress. It will assess the situation and begin to identify options for the post-July 2011 period. There will likely be three types of options that will dominate the minds of the Special Envoy Richard Holbrooke, Ambassador Karl Eikenberry, and the new military commander, General David Petraeus.

First, there will no doubt be some key players who favor continuing with the current U.S. plan that is still unfolding. Given the protracted nature of such conflicts, and barring unforeseen surprises, the battlefield situation in December 2010 is not likely to be radically different than it is now. Many, though certainly not all, conservatives will prefer to keep up the full-blown COIN operation for a few more years, and move slowly on the transition to Afghan responsibility for security and only then onto reconciliation with the enemy.

This would give the best breathing space needed for building Afghan capacity, but it is expensive and plays into enemy propaganda about the coalition as an occupying force. Moreover, this plan will entail very high expenditures, with no guarantee of results. If its proponents succeed, it will last only for a short time, perhaps as much as another year, up to the summer of 2012. Whatever the selected option, one aspect of the current plan that should be maintained is the progress that ISAF has made in protecting the population and showing respect to Afghans on the roads and in their homes. Allied restraint toward the civilian population has shown positive results, but there are some indications that restrictive rules of engagement (ROE) may also be affecting troop morale. General Petraeus indicated in his confirmation hearing that he would reexamine this problem and the existing ROE.

A second option would be to reduce over a year (July 2011-July 2012) most of the 30,000 Soldiers and Marines in the surge combat forces and make security assistance and capacity building—not the provision of combat forces—ISAF's top priority. Remaining ISAF combat units could further integrate with fielded ANA units. Maximum emphasis would be placed on quality training for soldiers and policemen. To build Afghan military capacity, ISAF commanders would also emphasize the development of Afghan combat enablers, such as logistics, transportation, and aviation. In this option, the focal point of allied strategy would be on the NATO Training Mission—Afghanistan, and not on allied combat forces. This training mission is still short permanent cadres and is being kept on track by hundreds of U.S. temporary-duty military personnel.

This option would not be cheap, but it could gradually bring down costs and troop levels. Trading U.S. combat units for ANA or integrated formations, however, would result in some short-term security degradation, a real problem if negotiations are ongoing. On the other hand, the integration of ISAF combat units with ANA units could also pay great training dividends in a few years.

There are other challenges that may arise with this option: The Afghan government may resist integration and improvements in unity of command. U.S. and allied trainer/advisor shortages will have to be filled rapidly. This will be difficult. In a similar vein, the training and education of Afghan civil servants will need much more attention, and additional trainer/advisors. In order to bring this about, the coalition needs also to reinforce support to the national government, its ministries, and its local appointees.

The biggest obstacle to success here is and will remain the Afghan police, who will be vital to success in defeating the insurgency. Efforts to improve their training must be increased. Rule-of-law programs — courts, jails, legal services — must also be improved if this government will ever rival Taliban dispute resolution mechanisms. The Ministry of Interior may well have to be broken up to defeat its endemic corrupt practices, which go all the way to the top levels of the ministry, according to in-country observers. The appointment of General Bismillah Khan Mohammadi, formerly chief of the General Staff, as the Minister of the Interior may provide an impetus for change.

For its part, the government of Afghanistan — which ultimately must win its own war — must work harder against corruption and redouble its efforts to develop its own capacity in every field of endeavor. Links between the center and the provinces must be strengthened. Coalition civilian advisors must become the norm in every ministry and throughout their subdivisions. The civilian part of the U.S. surge must clearly be maintained for a few more years.

A third option — compatible with the options noted above, either sequentially or concurrently — is for the Afghan government, with coalition and UN support, to move out smartly on reintegration of individuals and reconciliation with parts of or even the entire Afghan Taliban. To do this, President Karzai first will have to win over the nearly 60 percent of the Afghan population who are not Pashtuns. These groups — Tajiks, Uzbeks, Hazarras, and others — were treated poorly by the Taliban and today often live in areas outside Taliban influence. They will want peace, but not at a price that threatens their regions or allows the new Taliban much latitude.

There should be limits to coalition flexibility. Reconciliation and reintegration are not for war criminals. The Afghan constitution cannot be bargained away, and participants of all stripes must renounce violence, disavow al Qaeda, and come home to Afghanistan without arms. One downside here is the potential for simultaneous talking and fighting to take place. This is hard for Westerners to tolerate; authoritarian entities, like the Taliban, often can manipulate talk-fight periods to their advantage. The best way to ensure Taliban sincerity is to keep up constant military pressure on its formations and their command cadres. The more the Taliban feel the heat from the coalition and Pakistan, the more likely it will be to embrace reconciliation.

In sterile decisionmaking exercises, teams might well decide that the clear way ahead is to go through these options in order, starting with another dose of full-service COIN, with coincident reintegration of individual belligerents. This would be followed by Afghanization, with reconciliation beginning only after option two is well underway. Life, however, often defeats linear thinking. This is a time of rapid change on many fronts. The Coalition is in the same boat today as British Prime Minister Harold Macmillan was during the Cold War. When asked what his greatest challenges would be, Macmillan replied: "Events, my dear boy, events."[32]

Reconciliation, spurred by political maneuvering and war weariness may end up leading and not following developments on the battlefield. Counterinsurgency successes in Pakistan can change the battlefield dynamics in Afghanistan, and vice versa. Agreements among regional powers can effect military operations. The exploitation of mineral wealth may provide great incentives for some insurgents to come home and improve their economic lot.

There is an understandable reluctance to move into negotiations while the war continues. Few wars, however, end with the unconditional surrender of your enemy on the deck of a battleship, or with an evacuation of your diplomats as enemy tanks seize an ally's capital city. Most irregular and civil wars end in some form of negotiation. The United States should not stand in the way of reconciliation with the Taliban. Rather, it should work for the best possible outcome, guided both by its objectives and the available means.

The degree of help the coalition gets from Pakistan will be a key variable in any scenario. Indeed, increased Pakistani pressure on the Afghan Taliban could drastically speed up reconciliation. The United States must continue to insist that Pakistan take action against U.S. and Afghan enemies resident on its soil. To obtain the assistance of the regional powers, all of those powers must believe that a future Afghanistan will **not** work against their interests. To that end, an understanding between India and Pakistan on the future of Afghanistan will be critical to long-term stability in Afghanistan. Separate negotiations among regional powers may be as important as any of the above noted options. To facilitate these negotiations,

Special Representative Richard Holbrooke and his team should be given expanded authority to facilitate regional negotiations with all interested parties, to include India.

INTERIM RECOMMENDATIONS

It is not possible now to chart an exact course for the future. It may well be, that despite our best hopes, the war continues unabated. Security assistance may move to the forefront of the allied agenda. Reintegration of individuals and reconciliation with parts or all of the Taliban may occur much faster than the Western powers prefer. Regional actors, like Pakistan or Iran, may play more constructive roles in reaching settlements or otherwise fashioning a better peace.

While major outcomes are all wrapped in a fog of uncertainty, there are any number of key issues that the U.S. leadership team needs to tackle right away. First, on the military side of the house, it will be necessary to keep up the pressure on the Taliban. Protecting the population should remain the first priority, but one of the best ways to do that is to eliminate the Taliban, i.e., the forces which would oppress the population we seek to protect. If reconciliation advances, there will be many, including some in Afghanistan and Pakistan, who will want to cut back on offensive operations and counterterrorist activities against the Taliban. In truth, reconciliation in the long run depends on destroying Taliban formations and convincing them that reconciliation is a better path.

In a similar vein, there is the issue of rules of engagement. ISAF must balance protecting the population with the need to provide air and artillery support to its forces on the ground. It may well be that there is less here than meets the eye. It may also be that the ROE are fine, but are being misinterpreted in some units.

Secondly, it is clear that there needs to be better teamwork among our leadership in-country. If the change in military commanders does not help this situation, the President will have to take a more active role or appoint one of the three as *primus inter pares*, which is easier written than carried out. Iraq and Afghanistan are proof positive that personal chemistry can remove obstacles to cooperation, but that chemistry is not always there. It is not clear if you can legislate or even order such chemistry, but it may help to clarify intra-command relationships. On a brighter note, inside the operational elements in Afghanistan, civil-military cooperation has improved tremendously. The civilian surge is working, even if slower than some had hoped. Regional Command-East, for example, by the end of 2010, will have close to 300 civilian professionals to work with its military forces in their areas of responsibility, which constitute roughly a fourth of the country. There is now integration of politico-military efforts at the brigade, regional, and national levels.[33] Indeed, this is one area where the subordinates may be able to teach their superiors important lessons.

Finally, it is imperative that we focus on building Afghan capacity, not just in the short term in the national security ministries, but across the board in the long term in the civil government and private sectors. Training and advising are important in the short term, but in the long term we must think in decades about how to help Afghanistan help itself to overcome the horrendous effects of 32 years of war. Governance, rule of law, and basic enterprise management must all be reinforced. Improving Afghan colleges and graduate schools must be a high-priority activity for the long term. While a highly centralized government is not a good idea, and working more closely with local governments is important, it is also true that there will be no end to the problems of Afghanistan unless there is a functioning government in Kabul that is well linked into the provinces and districts and able to perform the basic security and welfare functions of a state.

The United States has preached for a decade in its advisory and development activities that teaching people to fish is better than providing them with fish. The truth of the matter is, however, that we are superb at providing fish and have not done well at teaching how to fish, which in this case means building capacity and mentoring Afghans. As we work on building national security and local defense forces, we need to redouble our efforts at building up Afghan human capital and the institutions of governance that one day will enable the state of Afghanistan to stand on its own two feet. If this does not come to pass, we will ultimately fail in Afghanistan.[34]

ENDNOTES - CHAPTER 7

1. President Barack Obama, "Remarks by the President in Address to the Nation on the Way Forward in Afghanistan and Pakistan," West Point, NY, December 1, 2009, available from *www.whitehouse.gov/the-press-office/remarks-president-address-nation-way-forward-afghanistan-and-pakistan*.

2. *Year of the Drone: An Analysis of U.S. Drone Strikes in Pakistan, 2004-10,* Washington, DC: New America Foundation, April 2010, available from *counterterrorism.newamerica.net/drones*. Obama administration data in this study was current to the end of March 2010.

3. The long-term relationship was discussed by both Secretary Hillary Rodham Clinton and President Hamid Karzai at an open meeting at the United States Institute of Peace, May 13, 2010. A transcript of this meeting is available from *www.state.gov/secretary/rm/2010/05/141825.htm* .

4. The best source on OEF casualties is available from *www.icasualties.org/oef/* .

5. General Kayani spoke at a by-invitation meeting at the New America Foundation, March 25, 2010.

6. Author's estimate, based on past spending patterns. Some unofficial estimates go as high as 100 billion dollars to be expended in Fiscal Year 2010.

7. Author conversation with a serving defense official, Spring 2010.

8. David Ignatius, "What Would Reconciliation Look Like for the U.S.," *Washington Post*, June 29, 2010, available from *www.washingtonpost.com/wp-dyn/content/article/2010/06/28/AR2010062802758.html?hpid%3Dopinionsbox1&sub=AR*. See also, unpublished testimony, General David Petraeus, to Senate Armed Services Committee, June 29, 2010.

9. Eric Schmitt, "U.S. Envoy's Cables Show Worries on Afghan Plans," *New York Times*, January 25, 2010, available from *www.nytimes.com/2010/01/26/world/asia/26strategy.html* .

10. Michael Hastings, "The Runaway General," *Rolling Stone*, June 22, 2010, available from *www.rollingstone.com/politics/news/17390/119236*.

11. Karzai *et al.*, USIP, May 13, 2010.

12. One of the better articles on the initial phases of OEF is by Stephen Biddle, "Afghanistan and the Future of Warfare," March-April 2003, available from *www.foreignaffairs.com/articles/58811/stephen-biddle/afghanistan-and-the-future-of-warfare* .

13. Secretary of Defense Donald Rumsfeld, "21st Century Defense Transformation of the U.S. Armed Forces," Speech at the National Defense University, January 31st, 2002, available from *www.defense.gov/speeches/speech.aspx?speechid=183*.

14. Various USAID web site articles, especially, *afghanistan. usaid.gov//en/Page.CountryOverview.aspx* . UN Human Development Reports and their Index are available from *hdr.undp.org/en/ statistics/*.

15. For a précis of Khalilzad's masterful performance in Afghanistan, see Kathleen Parker, "The U.S. can't ignore Karzai's Tantrum," *Washington Post*, April 11, 2010, available from *www.washingtonpost.com/wp-dyn/content/article/2010/04/09/ AR2010040904013.html*.

16. James Dobbins, *et al.*, *America's Role in Nation-Building: From Germany to Iraq*, Santa Monica, CA: 2003, pp. xviii, 157-159.

17. Unpublished U.S. Embassy derived statistics for the years 2002 to 2008. Those proportions in 2008 were reversed, with security assistance-related activities having two-thirds of the available dollars. The author thanks Ambassador William Wood for sharing this material.

18. This material represents the author's calculation, using U.S. Embassy statistics, 2002-08, and assuming a population of 29 million Afghans. These statistics do not include U.S. or international expenditures for their own military forces.

19. USAID statistics, available from *afghanistan.usaid.gov//en/ Page.CountryOverview.aspx* .

20. Unpublished Central Command statistics briefed at National Defense University in 2009.

21. ISAF statistics and visuals used in CSIS's Anthony Cordesman and Jason Lemieux, *Afghan Campaign: An Overview*, available from *csis.org/publication/afghan-war-campaign-overview-0* .

22. Testimony of former Under Secretary of State James K. Glassman before the Senate Foreign Relations Committee, March 10, 2010, available from *mountainrunner.us/files/congress/testimony/ SFRC_20100310-GlassmanTestimony100310p.pdf* .

23. Then-unpublished UN report cited in Agence France Presse dispatch, January 12, 2010, available from *www.google.com/hostednews/afp/article/ALeqM5g4utYst-DaAXPCnjeGyl2AMualJw*.

24. Unpublished ISAF J1 statistics briefed at the National War College, Spring 2010.

25. Conversations with various General Officers and CENTCOM and Joint Staff planners, 2003-04.

26. This conclusion was strongly influenced by the year-by-year ABC News-BBC and Asia Foundation polling. Somewhat mysteriously, the trends noted above showed a sharp positive increase in the 2009 ABC-BBC polls, before the U.S. surge and coincident with the first round of Presidential elections. The 2009 polls are available from *abcnews.go.com/images/PollingUnit/1099a1Afghanistan-WhereThingsStand.pdf* and *www.asiafoundation.org/resources/pdfs/Afghanistanin2009.pdf* .

27. Conversations between the author and two senior NSC officials, as well as a scholar who later participated in the review, Spring 2010.

28. *White Paper of the Interagency Policy Group's Report on U.S. Policy toward Afghanistan and Pakistan*, March 27, 2009, available from *www.whitehouse.gov/assets/documents/Afghanistan-Pakistan_White_Paper.pdf*. The short quote is on page 6.

29. General Stanley A. McChrystal, USA, COMISAF's Initial Assessment (Redacted), August 30, 2009, available from *media.washingtonpost.com/wp-srv/politics/documents/Assessment_Redacted_092109.pdf*.

30. President Barack Obama, "Remarks by the President in Address to the Nation on the Way Forward in Afghanistan and Pakistan," West Point, NY, December 1, 2009, available from *www.whitehouse.gov/the-press-office/remarks-president-address-nation-way-forward-afghanistan-and-pakistan*.

31. *Ibid.*

32. Quoted in "Harold MacMillan," Wikipedia, available from *en.wikipedia.org/wiki/Harold_Macmillan*.

33. See interview with Major General Mike Scaparrotti, USA, the commander of Regional Command-East, June 3, 2010, available from *www.defense.gov/transcripts/transcript.aspx?transcriptid=4628* . Scaparrotti and his civilian deputy, Dawn Liberi, noted that there would be nearly 300 civilian experts in the command by the end of 2010. A recently returned commander of an airborne brigade in that region spoke in the Spring of 2010 to a National Defense Univeristy (NDU) audience regarding the unity of effort on stability operations and reconstruction that takes place at every level of command.

34. This paragraph is an edited version of part of a letter to the editor on Afghanistan issues in *Joint Force Quarterly*, Vol. 58, 3d Quarter, July 2010.

CHAPTER 8

STABILIZATION AND RECONSTRUCTION IN
CONFLICT AND POST-CONFLICT SINCE 9/11

James Stephenson

INTRODUCTION

In the fall of 2001, approximately 100 Central Intelligence Agency (CIA) operatives and 300 Special Operations forces drove the Taliban and al Qaeda from Afghanistan in a little over 2 months. In 8 years, almost 1,000 American lives and $200 billion later, we will soon have a U.S. military force of 98,000 and a $38-billion foreign-assistance program arrayed against a resurgent Taliban that effectively controls large swaths of Afghanistan.[1] Our ally and exit strategy, the Karzai government, is corrupt, largely viewed by Afghans as illegitimate and by virtually all as massively ineffective at delivering essential services and governance to its constituents. To the east, our fickle ally, Pakistan, is also corrupt and impoverished; is a sanctuary to the Taliban, al Qaeda, and a stew of other Afghan insurgents; is unstable; and is perched atop a stockpile of nuclear weapons. Having gained little from billions of dollars of military and foreign assistance over the last 8 years, the United States just promised Pakistan an additional $7.5 billion in foreign aid, in addition to a continuation of high levels of military assistance. One could argue that our position is precarious. How we got there is a cautionary tale worth telling in the hope that we can right our course and avoid the missteps of the past.

THE PERVERSE IMPACT OF IRAQ RECONSTRUCTION

U.S. Secretary of Defense Donald Rumsfeld clearly did not want the armed forces to engage in nation building in Afghanistan, but when the Department of State and the U.S. Agency for International Development (USAID) arrived in the wake of the Taliban defeat, the Pentagon was appalled at their paucity of personnel and financial resources. The response of the Pentagon was not to militarize foreign assistance to the then-peaceful Afghanistan, but angst over the State and USAID approach did lead Secretary Rumsfeld to demand that the Department of Defense (DoD) be responsible not only for the 2003 invasion of Iraq, but also for any post-war reconstruction. National Security Presidential Directive (NSPD) 24 gave Rumsfeld the authority he sought. Although USAID was brought into the late-stage planning at the DoD, the State Department was closed out and largely ignored. To manage post-war Iraq reconstruction, the DoD created the Office of Reconstruction and Humanitarian Assistance (ORHA), which was made up of a handful of retired officers, DoD civilians, USAID officers, and, reluctantly, several officers seconded from State. ORHA was a modest effort, whose leadership was convinced that the major post-war risk was humanitarian suffering, and that its mission would conclude in a matter of a few months. USAID was, however, allowed to plan for a longer-term stabilization and reconstruction program, drawing on its experience in other post-conflict countries, most recently the Balkans and the former East Bloc. As it was, ORHA had barely reached Baghdad, Iraq, when it was unceremoniously informed of its demise and the succession of the Coalition Provisional Authority (CPA) led by Ambassador L. Paul Bremer III, reporting to the Secretary of Defense. There was nothing modest about the CPA. Although it initially had only a few billion dollars of appropriated funding for reconstruction inherited from ORHA, the CPA, fueled by DoD hiring, quickly grew to some 4,000 souls—at the time, nearly four times larger than USAID's entire Foreign Service.[2] The Pentagon was in charge, and its approach to reconstruction was to go big. It was going to rebuild Iraq, and then hand it back to the Iraqis and leave. Seated in Baghdad, the CPA quickly opened regional offices to reach into every province of Iraq. Senior Advisors and staff were assigned to every government ministry as surrogates. Ambassador Bremer was the legal and de facto leader of Iraq and issued general orders to effect his authority.

Although the CPA had a statement of broad goals for rebuilding Iraq, it never had a coherent strategy with carefully phased activities to achieve objectives. Instead, it tried to do everything at once. CPA personnel, often hired for their political loyalty, served for as little as 3 months, and typically had no prior experience in stabilization and reconstruction. USAID was reduced to an executing agency, with little input in program decisionmaking. Much of the plan it had developed under ORHA was either abandoned or gutted of funding to bolster other CPA priorities. By July 2003, it was clear that the CPA was going to need more money, a lot more money, and Bremer ordered his staff to prepare a reconstruction plan and budget to be sent to Congress. Developed in the span of a few weeks, the $18.4 billion plan that went to Congress was heavily focused on rebuilding physical infrastructure—electricity, water, sewerage, oil, transportation, communications, rail, hospitals, schools, and security. To foreign assistance professionals, it was a staggeringly extravagant program that ignored the hard-learned lessons from 50 years of foreign aid, but $18.4 billion was pocket change to the DoD.

Stabilization and reconstruction is an enabling process that follows a critical path dictated by political, economic, social, and physical forces often outside the control of the practitioners. It is rarely about simply rebuilding a country's physical infrastructure. The CPA's tenure in Iraq was doomed by Iraqi desire and demand for self-determination. Before the ink was dry on the $18.4 billion supplemental appropriation, the Bush administration was forced to agree that the CPA would end on June 30, 2004, and hand sovereignty back to a transitional Iraqi government. The CPA would be replaced by an embassy. Unfortunately, the painful transition from DoD/CPA control to State control, mandated by NSPD 36, was heavily influenced by the extant, unprecedented structures of the CPA and the inherited $18.4 billion plan. The transition negotiations between State and the DoD resulted in an American Embassy, albeit smaller than the CPA, but still the largest in the world. The CPA reconstruction program was realigned to provide more funding for democracy, governance, agriculture, civil society, and economic growth, but remained heavily tilted toward physical infrastructure. Although more effort was made to enable Iraqis to rebuild their own country, the original design of the CPA program determined a course that had the U.S. Government still attempting to rebuild it for them. At the time, no one knew the adjustment to an inherited, ill-conceived program for Iraq would reverberate for so long or so profoundly. Afghanistan, which was then a backwater, was destined for a makeover.

STABILIZATION, RECONSTRUCTION, AND EXPEDITIONARY CIVILIANS

Stabilization is the process of establishing enough governance, security, and economic activity to enable the process of reconstruction, which is the longer-term rebuilding of institutions of civil society, governance, security, and the economy. In Iraq, reconstruction was begun before stabilization was achieved. Stabilization has to be highly visible, and this militates towards many small community projects, including ones that promote entrepreneurship and enable the creation of small and micro enterprises that marginally improve people's lives. Stabilization buys time for reconstruction, which takes longer and may be largely invisible to the average citizen. By concentrating on large infrastructure, which is capital intensive and takes years to complete, the CPA squandered the opportunity to convince the average Iraqi that his life was going to be better. Iraqi disappointment and frustration fed the insurgency. Even the U.S forces — who joked that CPA stood for "Can't Provide Anything" — quickly learned of the need for visible stabilization efforts. The Commander's Emergency Response Program (CERP) became the vehicle for maneuver units to engage in thousands of projects at the community level. It was not perfect, and the quality of implementation varied with the expertise of the officer dispensing it, but CERP addressed a void that anyone on the ground could see. USAID also implemented community development projects, but its program was initially constrained by funding decisions of the CPA. The realignment enabled USAID to dedicate $400 million to economic policy, market reform, and private-sector development, as well as greater efforts at the community level to enable an environment for Iraqi's to improve their quality of life and for entrepreneurs to either start or expand small enterprises.

In Afghanistan, State and USAID embarked on an effort to build a strong central government from the top down, where none had ever effectively governed. Stabilization was never achieved. The U.S. program was Kabul-centric, with most Afghans oblivious to any efforts to improve their lives. No community development efforts were undertaken, in spite of the success of the World Bank National Solidarity Program, which enabled thousands of projects in rural villages. Recognizing the problem, the Coalition began in 2003 to form Provincial Reconstruction Teams (PRTs), military units with civilian advisors from State, US-AID, and the Department of Agriculture, tasked with working with local governments to implement relatively small projects. While the PRTs met with some success, performance and methods were decidedly mixed. USAID initially staffed most PRTs with a single personal services contractor, while State tended to use junior Foreign Service officers. PRTs were also severely limited in their effect in southern and eastern Afghanistan by the security challenges of movement in a hostile environment. In spite of the limitations, State decided in 2005 to build PRTs in Iraq, where they also were hampered by deteriorating security and, again, had modest impact. PRTs are deeply resented by nongovernmental organizations (NGOs) operating in the same space, who argue that military personnel delivering the same assistance creates identity confusion and makes targets of the NGOs, which have traditionally been viewed as neutral and accorded humanitarian space. The more salient point is that

NGOs, unlike PRTs, generally use local nationals to continually engage communities and local governments. PRTs typically engage a community by arriving in an armed military convoy. Often they are unable to leave their bases for weeks at a time, due to security threats. Essentially military units with a few civilian advisors, the PRTs in Afghanistan generally have 80-100 personnel. Given that the cost of deploying a soldier to Afghanistan is $1 million a year, PRTs are an enormous investment for very little return.[3]

By 2004, senior members of Congress and the Bush administration, alarmed at the poor mobilization and implementation of the reconstruction efforts in Afghanistan and Iraq, sought a mechanism within the U.S. Government to better plan for and implement stabilization and reconstruction, utilizing the full range of the government's civilian assets, when necessary in coordination with U.S. military forces. While legislation did not pass until 2009, the State Department created the Office of the Coordinator for Reconstruction and Stabilization (S/CRS) in 2004 as the operational component of the State Department's reconstruction and stabilization (R&S) activities. S/CRS is charged by Congress and the Secretary of State with building and maintaining an expeditionary, innovative, and interagency civilian capability to plan, manage, and conduct U.S. stabilization operations on behalf of the Secretary of State and Chiefs of Mission overseas.[4] It is tasked with cooperating closely with the DoD, but its limited funding and staff are dwarfed by the military's capabilities. S/CRS has had only a marginal role in Afghanistan and Iraq.

S/CRS seeks to monitor countries at risk of failure and maintain a small Standby Component of interagency professionals prepared to deploy in Advance

Civilian Teams anywhere in the world within days. It is building a Civilian Response Corps (CRC) of interagency professionals to deploy within 30-60 days to support the advance teams. The planned CRC of up to 5,000 private citizens with critical skills has not been funded by Congress. While persons in the Standby Component and Civilian Response Corps have deployed as individuals to address specific needs, and assessment teams have performed discrete missions in support of country teams, to date, S/CRS has deployed no Advance Civilian Teams to manage stabilization and reconstruction efforts. Indeed, State has used S/CRS and the CRC to staff the needs of ad hoc efforts, e.g., the Special Representative for Afghanistan and Pakistan.[5]

Even as S/CRS sought to establish itself as *the* coordinator of U.S. Government stabilization efforts, it has endured constant criticism and attack from various quarters. The Special Inspector General for Iraq Reconstruction (SIGIR) recently proposed creating the U.S. Office of Contingency Operations, which would absorb S/CRS and parts of USAID and other agencies and report to the National Security Advisor. The staff of the Senate Foreign Relations Committee is circulating draft legislation that would terminate S/CRS and create a joint State-USAID office, reporting directly to the Secretary of State. These efforts are indicative of the lack of confidence within the government that S/CRS will ever be capable of performing its expeditionary mission.

Skepticism of S/CRS appears to be strongest at the DoD, which embraced stabilization and reconstruction—what the military calls Stability Operations—in 2005 with the Defense Directive 3000.05, which raised stability operations to the same level of importance as combat operations. It states that, "stability opera-tions tasks are best performed by indigenous, foreign or U.S. civilian professionals," but, "nonetheless, U.S. military forces shall be prepared to perform all tasks necessary to establish or maintain order when civil-ians cannot do so." It also directs the Deputy Secretary of Defense for Personnel and Readiness to develop, "methods to recruit, select and assign current and for-mer DoD personnel with relevant skills for service in stability operations assignments."[6] In 2008, the Army issued its first *Field Manual for Stability Operations* (*FM 3-07*), and is becoming increasingly sophisticated at stabilization and reconstruction. In 2007, exercises in stability operations were incorporated into Mission Readiness Exercises for all brigades deploying to Af-ghanistan and Iraq. In theater, U.S. forces are experi-menting with methodologies that use development experts and indigenous personnel to engage with communities and traditional governance structures. While U.S. Secretary of Defense Robert Gates has been an outspoken advocate for funding the S/CRS Civilian Reserve Corps, he has nevertheless ordered the DoD to build its own Civilian Expeditionary Workforce, and that effort is underway. Finally, the *Capstone Con-cept for Joint Operations*, which seeks to envisage how the joint forces will operate in the future and in what environments, recognizes relief and reconstruction as a key component of how joint forces will operate. It was signed by the Chairman of the Joint Chiefs of Staff in January 2009.[7]

THE SHRINKING OF USAID

USAID's slow slide toward the abyss accelerated during the Clinton administration as Congress cut USAID's operating budget, compelling it to reduce its force of Foreign Service Officers. To compensate and continue to perform its mission, USAID increasingly utilized personal services contractors, many of whom were retired or involuntarily separated former Foreign Service Officers. These positions could be salaried with program funds, which, contrary to the operating budget, continued to grow. The second blow was the administration's innovation of inviting other departments and agencies of the government to encroach on the foreign-assistance program. It was the nascence of what would later be heralded as "a whole-of-government approach." The Departments of Treasury and Justice not only carved out swaths of foreign assistance, but asserted their ownership of what they had taken. The Departments of Commerce and Agriculture strengthened their own foreign-assistance services and participation in foreign-assistance programs. The Department of State reserved more Economic Support Funds for its own use. At the same time, Congress began to mandate State Department Coordinators for special-assistance programs in the Balkans and former Soviet states. Increasingly, these coordinators not only made policy, but dictated the method of implementation and dispersed funding. USAID's share of funding and influence diminished, in Washington and overseas. Faced with shrinking power, influence, and operating budgets, USAID shed many of its specialized officers in health, education, engineering, and science, and relied more and more on obtaining those skills by contract from the private sector. In some countries, missions were closed because USAID simply did not have sufficient operating funds to keep them open. The end of the 1990s seemed like the nadir for USAID. The next decade was worse.

The George W. Bush administration's disastrous venture with the ad hoc Coalition Provisional Authority did not sway it from other ventures. Instead, it continued to diminish USAID by creating new institutions to implement large elements of foreign assistance that had traditionally been the province of USAID. In 2003, President Bush created the President's Emergency Plan for AIDS Relief (PEPFAR), a 5-year, $15-billion initiative managed by a Global AIDS Coordinator reporting to the Secretary of State.[8] USAID was but one of a half-dozen agencies tasked with its implementation. In 2008, PEPFAR was renewed until 2013, increased to a commitment of $48 billion and expanded to cover other infectious diseases, further eroding USAID's health portfolio. In 2004, the President created the Millennium Challenge Corporation (MCC) to form partnerships with some of the world's poorest countries and provide large-scale grants to fund country-led solutions for reducing poverty through sustainable economic growth.[9] To date, the MCC has signed compacts with 20 countries for $7 billion. As of July 2008, it has disbursed only $235 million of the $7.5 billion provided by Congress.[10] The MCC tends to be popular with conservative think-tanks as an innovative approach to foreign assistance, but has been criticized by development professionals and Congress for slow implementation and questionable achievements. However, the MCC has been embraced by the Obama administration, and Congress continues to provide it with funding, though at levels significantly below the administration's requests.

The Bush administration's worst blow to USAID occurred in 2006, when it appointed Randall L. Tobias as the first U.S. Director of Foreign Assistance, to serve concurrently as the Administrator of USAID. Tobias was responsible for overseeing all foreign-assistance activities of the U.S. Government. In addition to his direct responsibilities for USAID, Tobias was charged with directing the transformation of the U.S. Government's approach to foreign-assistance. Responsible for providing strategic direction and guidance to all other foreign-assistance programs delivered through the various agencies and entities of the U.S. Government, including MCC and the Global AIDS Coordinator, he reported directly to the Secretary of State and held the rank of Deputy Secretary of State. USAID was stripped of its policy, program, and coordination functions, which were moved to the Department of State.[11] The "F process," launched by U.S. Secretary of State Condoleezza Rice in January 2006, was designed to place USAID under more direct control of the State Department.[12] The new F Bureau, staffed by State and USAID personnel, was tasked with integrating foreign-assistance planning and resource management across State and USAID. This radically altered the relationship between USAID, the State Department, and Congress. USAID no longer submitted its annual budget request directly to the Office of Management and Budget. Instead, The F process integrated USAID programs into the foreign operations budget request of the Department of State. USAID had lost it voice in policy, and no longer controlled either its budget or the programming of it.

These events spawned alarm in the development community, Congress, and think tanks. Numerous studies were published, most arguing for the rebuilding of USAID capabilities and its autonomy. Some went so far as to argue that USAID's authorities and independence be restored and it be elevated to a Cabinet-level department. Others argued for abolishing USAID and rewriting the Foreign Assistance Act of 1961. Still others argued for absorbing USAID into the Department of State. No consensus had been reached by the inauguration of the Obama administration, though the weight of opinion in the development community seemed to favor a return of USAID's authorities and autonomy, at least to the *status quo ante*, and a significant increase in personnel. The confirmation of Hillary Clinton as Secretary of State was warmly greeted by the development community, given her foreign affairs credentials and her long history of support for foreign aid and USAID. Clinton spoke of "smart power" and the "three D's of Diplomacy, Defense and Development."[13] Many thought that the pursuit of these concepts heralded the elevation of USAID. They were soon disabused. For 11 months, while no nomination was forthcoming, USAID was led by a career officer, supervised by the Deputy Secretary of State for Management and Resources. No authorities were returned to USAID. Secretary Clinton did support and win funding for significant increases in USAID and State personnel. She spoke often of her desire to strengthen USAID, but also spoke of the need for diplomacy and development to serve policy and be closely coordinated. It appeared to many that the USAID the Secretary supported was one she envisioned either within the Department of State or closely supervised by it. The Secretary remained ambiguous, if not opaque, about her intentions.

In July 2009, Secretary Clinton announced the *Quadrennial Diplomacy and Development Review* (QDDR), a "process to guide us to agile, responsive, and effective institutions of diplomacy and development, including how to transition from approaches no longer commensurate with current challenges," and, "offer guidance on how we develop policies; how we allocate our resources; how we deploy our staff; and how we exercise our authorities."[14] In August 2009, President Obama signed a Presidential Study Directive (PSD-7), ordering an interagency review of all U.S. global development policy, led by the National Security Council and National Economic Council. This seemed unprecedented, coming only months after the QDDR was announced, and was widely viewed as a slap at the more parochial QDDR. It came after Senators John Kerry and Dick Lugar introduced the Foreign Assistance Revitalization and Accountability Act (S.1524) to rebuild the USAID and strengthen evaluation of foreign-aid programs. Finally, under increased scrutiny for his failure to nominate a new USAID administrator, President Obama announced the nomination of Rajiv Shah to lead the Agency. At his confirmation hearing on December 1, 2009, Shah testified, "Not since the founding of USAID in 1961 and the passage of the Foreign Assistance Act have we had such an opportunity to fundamentally re-imagine our nation's development strategy and strengthen the organization that leads it."[15] Just weeks later, Shah was tapped by President Obama to lead U.S. efforts to respond to the devastating earthquake in Haiti, and Shah received high marks for his performance; however, Secretary Clinton put her Chief of Staff, Cheryl Mills, in charge of all funding decisions, raising questions about who was really in charge.

Perhaps no one but President Obama knows what the convergence of the QDDR, PSD-7, and congressional efforts will produce with regard to the future of USAID and U.S. foreign assistance. The publication of the results of the QDDR has been delayed, and the National Security Council (NSC) has reportedly agreed to hold the publication of the PSD review until after the release of the QDDR, though a draft summary of the PSD-7 recommendations was leaked in April 2010. It is reasonable to assume, though not certain, that Congress will hold off on bringing S.1524 to the floor until both the QDDR and PSD results are officially released. In the meantime, there are signs that the State Department continues to extend its influence over USAID and foreign assistance, both in Washington and the field. For example, the State Department's International Cooperative Administrative Support Services initiative to consolidate administrative services at U.S. embassies worldwide, according to a March 2010 survey by the American Foreign Service Association, rather than being used to increase efficiency and reduce costs, is being used instead to force USAID to utilize incompatible, less efficient, more costly systems of the State Department. The authors of the survey concluded that "USAID's ability to support its staff and carry out its development goals overseas is in serious jeopardy."[16] Nowhere is USAID's subordination to the State Department more evident than in Afghanistan and Pakistan (AFPAK).

AFGHANISTAN AND PAKISTAN

On January 22, 2009, just 2 days into the Obama administration, Secretary Clinton announced the appointment of Richard Holbrooke as the Special Representative for Afghanistan and Pakistan. Stating that nowhere was "the need for a vigorous diplomatic approach more apparent than in the two regions that epitomize the nuance and complexity of our interconnected world," she acknowledged that many "Foreign Service and Civil Service and Foreign National colleagues have been engaged on behalf of issues related to the Middle East and to Afghanistan and Pakistan for years, sometimes, as we know, at great peril and personal sacrifice," and promised their work would "continue to be the underpinning of everything our government does to achieve peace and stability in these regions." She went on to state that Mr. Holbrooke's task would be to "coordinate across the entire government an effort to achieve [the] United States' strategic goals in the region. This effort will be closely coordinated, not only within the State Department and, of course, with USAID, but also with the Defense Department and under the coordination of the National Security Council."[17]

In the ensuing months, it became clear that Mr. Holbrooke was far more than a coordinator of strategic goals. Within a few months, the country team in Afghanistan was reorganized and included, in addition to the Ambassador, a Deputy Ambassador and a Coordinating Director for Development and Economic Affairs, to whom the USAID Mission Director reported. (USAID Mission Directors normally report to the Ambassador). In Pakistan, the USAID Mission Director was replaced with a USAID officer known to Mr. Holbrooke from the Balkans. In August, former ambassador Robin Raphel was appointed to the Embassy in Islamabad as the State Department's non-military aid coordinator for Pakistan. Mr. Holbrooke announced that his team would develop an assistance strategy for both Afghanistan and Pakistan that, in a departure from USAID's normal operating modality, would utilize fewer U.S. contractors and NGOs; disburse funds directly to government entities, local contractors and NGOs; and significantly increase the number of U.S. Government employees in both countries, to directly implement the strategy. By the year's end, the U.S. Government civilian presence in Afghanistan tripled to almost 1,000, most ostensibly to be placed outside of Kabul in PRTs, District Support Teams, and with military maneuver units. In Pakistan, USAID was completely reorganized to implement the new strategy, though significant USAID staff increases were slower to be realized.

It is too soon to know whether the new strategies for Afghanistan and Pakistan will be successful, but there are a number of factors inherent to both countries and the AFPAK approach that raise concerns. The Transparency International Corruption Perceptions Index ranks Afghanistan as the world's second most corrupt country, at 179. Pakistan fairs slightly better with a score of 139, but still with a score of only 2.4 out of a possible 10.[18] Given endemic corruption in both government and the private sector, the plan to disburse funds directly to both governments and to local contractors and NGOs would seem fraught with the risk of both failure and the theft of funding. The use of U.S. contractors and NGOs, who hire local personnel and utilize local contractors and NGOs, provides the U.S. Government with a form of insurance. When U.S. contractors or NGOs fail to meet the terms of their agreements or lose funds due to fraud, waste, or abuse, they usually settle without legal action, but may be easily pursued in U.S. Federal Court. They are responsible and liable for the actions of their subcontractors and grantees. When they are removed and the U.S. Government enters into contractual relationships directly with foreign governments, contractors and NGOs, recourse is through local courts and processes with little chance of recovering funds lost, embezzled, or simply wasted.

Stabilization and reconstruction, particularly in dangerous environments, is an art traditionally practiced by a small cadre of experienced officers from State, USAID, a handful of other agencies, and a handful of contractors and NGOs. The business model being pursued by AFPAK, particularly in Afghanistan, requires larger numbers of experienced personnel than are available in either USAID or the State Department. Both have resorted to temporary hires, but many of these are reported to have not only no stabilization and reconstruction experience, but also no overseas development experience. Only a few State Department Foreign Service officers are trained and experienced to do stabilization and reconstruction. To expect temporary hires—essentially personal services contractors—to successfully engage in an effort so complex after a few months of training is unrealistic, if not dangerous. That would be the case in a permissive environment, which Afghanistan and Pakistan decidedly do not provide. Even before the civilian surge to Afghanistan, the security environment prevented PRT personnel and embassy personnel from providing adequate oversight to field activities. In dangerous environments, the State Department's security protocols, which cover USAID, place crippling restrictions on mobility, usually for valid reasons. USAID contractors and NGOs do not fall under those restrictions. While they must take extraordinary care to protect their personnel, they are generally adept at successfully performing their tasks, which involve operating outside the wire. This reality is borne out by the increased use of U.S. NGOs and contractors in Afghanistan in the past year, in spite of State Department claims to the contrary.

Since the Embassy bombings in Kenya and Tanzania in 1998, security considerations — including Inman-compliant buildings, armored vehicles, bodyguards, static guard forces, and secure communications — have greatly increased the costs of fielding Embassy staff. While there is no argument that both the State Department and USAID, particularly the latter, need significant increases in Foreign Service staff to meet global challenges, there is also no argument that it is costly. Embassy facilities will have to be expanded or new ones built. If the cost of fielding a single soldier for 1 year in Afghanistan is $1 million, what is the cost of fielding a single Foreign Service officer there? It is certainly no less, and a lot more than the cost of fielding an individual working for a contractor or NGO. Personnel numbers at USAID and the State Department declined over the past decades because Congress was not disposed to provide the funding to maintain them. Absent the national security threat that conditions in Afghanistan and Pakistan pose, what is the likelihood that Congress will continue to provide funding for expanded personnel numbers, much less the capacity to surge large numbers of personnel to the next threat? Is the AFPAK business model even sustainable?

A LEANER, SUSTAINABLE MODEL

The United States actually has in its recent history a successful model of how to fight a counterinsurgency: El Salvador. When that conflict flared in the late 1970s, the searing experience of Vietnam was fresh, and Congress was deeply skeptical of U.S. involvement in another guerilla war. President Reagan — determined to check communist expansion in Central America, but faced with stiff opposition in

Congress—agreed to limit military intervention to a Milgroup of 55 advisors who would train and equip the El Salvador Armed Forces (ESAF).[19] The Milgroup advisors, many of whom were Special Forces highly trained in counterinsurgency, were not allowed to accompany into combat the forces they trained. ESAF officers were also trained in the United States, and for a brief period Salvadoran soldiers were trained at a base in neighboring Honduras. Congressional opposition also contributed to keeping in check the number of State, USAID, and other personnel assigned to the Embassy in San Salvador. (At the peak, USAID had only 36 Foreign Service officers in-country, and approximately an equal number of personal services contractors working alongside.) Although Milgroup bridled at the inefficiencies of the limitations, they turned out to be a blessing.[20] Unable to go big, so to speak, Milgroup was forced to invest time, intelligence, equipment, and training to enable the ESAF to defeat the insurgency, not to do it for them. It took 12 years. While the ESAF was slowly becoming proficient, State and USAID worked with the government and civil society to enable reform of the social, economic and political system that had fueled the insurgency. Most significantly, USAID worked with the Salvadoran private sector to create organizations that supported entrepreneurs in the creation or expansion of micro, small, medium, and large enterprises in agriculture, services, industry, and export. Technical assistance and credit enabled the process. With USAID assistance, economist Dr. Arnold Harberger of the University of Chicago, and his team of Chicago Boys were brought in by The Salvadoran Foundation for Economic and Social Development (FUSADES) to design and help implement a comprehensive neoliberal economic reform program. This program, with the bottom-up enabling efforts, became the engine of economic recovery and sustained growth in gross domestic product (GDP). Community development programs empowered villagers and undermined the influence of the Farabundo Martí National Liberation Front (FMLN, the Marxist insurgency). Again, this was not a linear process, but one of steady progress with frequent setbacks. Undoubtedly, the breakup of the Soviet Union, which removed significant materiel support for the insurgents, helped, but by the beginning of peace negotiations in 1990, El Salvador was a different country than it had been in 1980. When the war ended by negotiation in 1992, the former FMLN insurgents, through peaceful elections the next year, became the loyal opposition in the legislature. In 2009, an FMLN candidate won the presidential elections, and there was a peaceful transition of power. El Salvador remains a peaceful democracy with a free market economy. The cost of victory to the United States was approximately $4 billion and a score of civilian and military casualties.

The model the United States employed in the countries of the former East-Bloc and the Balkans also utilized small numbers of highly qualified personnel with significant monetary resources at their disposal. Originally, the State Department wanted only a single USAID affairs officer in each embassy, but later recognized it needed USAID Missions. None of these were particularly robust. (For example, the USAID Mission in Serbia and Montenegro had only seven Foreign Service officers and nine personal service contractors to manage a fully integrated development program that averaged $200 million per year.) As in the case of El Salvador, the modalities used by State and USAID

161

were at least partly driven by decades of declining operating budgets and consequent reductions in personnel. This was particularly acute at USAID, whose corps of Foreign Service officers by the late-1990s had been reduced to just over 1,000. USAID had always utilized contractors and NGOs to implement foreign-assistance programs, but the declines in personnel meant that the ratio of program managers to contracts and grants widened significantly. Still, the model of enabling countries to reform and rebuild themselves, rather than doing it for them, was served well by relatively modest numbers of capable, experienced Foreign Service officers leveraged by contractors and NGOs that also used small numbers of expatriate personnel and larger numbers of local nationals. During the author's tenure in Iraq from 2004-05, the USAID Mission had 102 expatriates and 103 Iraqi nationals to manage a program of $5 billion with 9,000 projects. USAID's 50 contractors and NGOs employed daily as many as 70,000 Iraqis, though over half were day workers. The program during that period is generally conceded to have functioned well, and the Agency never wanted or asked for additional personnel. Success at post-conflict transition or counterinsurgency is predicated on the right enabling strategy, implemented by experienced practitioners with time and patience. Throwing more money and personnel at a bad strategy is a waste of both, as are misguided efforts to try to force a timeline that cannot be forced.

RATIONAL NATIONAL SECURITY REFORM

The Foreign Assistance Revitalization and Accountability Act (S.1524), as written, would restore USAID's policy and planning and strengthen its human resource capacity, but is ambiguous with regard to its authority over its own budget. If USAID's budget remains under the control of the Department of State, its influence and capability will continue to decline. In that event, the recommendation of the Special Inspector General for Iraq Reconstruction for the creation of the U.S. Office for Contingency Operations may be the most viable option for reforming U.S. capacity to conduct stabilization and reconstruction abroad. However, if the absorption of USAID by the Department of State is reversed, by legislation or executive action, USAID should also be designated as the coordinator of U.S. Government stabilization and reconstruction operations. Should that occur, a number of concurrent actions should be initiated.

USAID's Bureau of Democracy, Conflict, and Humanitarian Assistance should be expanded by folding its Office of Military Affairs, Office of Transition Initiatives, and Office of Civilian Response into a new Bureau of Stabilization and Reconstruction (BSR). S/CRS should be abolished and its responsibilities and functions transferred to the BSR, which would have interagency staffing from State, the DoD, and other agencies, including Senior Foreign Service and General Officer supervisory positions. BSR staffing in Washington should be only as large as necessary to monitor failed and failing states, plan for contingency operations, and maintain the capacity to field two Advance Civilian Teams simultaneously, anywhere in the world. The Standby Component in Washington should be supplemented by offering modest pay incentives to 500 qualified State and USAID Foreign Service officers, wherever serving, willing to deploy on 24 hours notice for up to a year. Members of a reduced 300-member Civilian Response Corps, drawn from other federal agencies, should receive the same incentive payments. The Civilian Reserve Corps should be abandoned. Continuous training should be provided to all BSR officers and reserves, including training with the military to develop stabilization and reconstruction skills. BSR and the military should develop flexible models for civilian-military cooperation in the field, but not be wedded to any single model, including the use of U.S. contractors and NGOs and their local employees.

Finally, stabilization and reconstruction operations are different than USAID's other development assistance operations and the Department of State's normal diplomatic postings. Officers attracted to stabilization and reconstruction are a different breed than those attracted to more normal postings. The fact is that stabilization and reconstruction are most often practiced in dangerous environments, under primitive living and working conditions. It is not for everyone. Both USAID and the Department of State should develop a cadre of officers with the inclination and skills for stabilization and reconstruction and cease the practice of requiring all officers to bid (volunteer) for assignments to countries where the United States is engaged in stabilization and reconstruction. The civilians who do stability and reconstruction are as different from the rest as Special Operations forces are from the rest of the military. In fact, they are very much like special operations forces and operate in the same environments — they just do it unarmed.

ENDNOTES - CHAPTER 8

1. "Afghanistan: U.S. Foreign Assistance," Washington, DC: Congressional Research Service, July 14, 2009, available from *fas. org/sgp/crs/row/R40699.pdf*.

2. Personnel reporting by the DoD on the numbers deployed to the CPA was so poor that no exact number is attainable.

3. Christopher Drew, "High Costs Weigh on Troop Debate for Afghan War," *New York Times*, November 14, 2009, available from *www.nytimes.com/2009/11/15/us/politics/15cost.html*.

4. Office of the Coordinator for Reconstruction and Stabilization, available from *www.state.gov/s/crs/index.htm*.

5. Office of the Coordinator for Reconstruction and Stabilization, available from *www.crs.state.gov/index.cfm?fuseaction=public. display&shortcut=JDKH*.

6. Department of Defense Directive 3000.05, Washington, DC, available from *www.usaid.gov/policy/cdie/sss06/sss_1_080106_dod. pdf*.

7. U.S. Joint Forces Command (USJFCOM), *available from www.jfcom.mil/new*.

8. President's Emergency Plan for AIDS Relief, available from *www.pepfar.gov/about/index.htmslink/storyarchive/2009/pa012309a. html*.

9. Millennium Challenge Corporation, available from *www. mcc.gov/mcc/about/index.shtml*.

10. Noam Unger and Margaret L. Taylor, "Capacity for Change, Reforming U.S. Assistance Efforts in Poor and Fragile Countries," Washington, DC: The Brookings Institution and the Center for Strategic and International Studies (CSIS), April 2010, p. 12.

11. *Ibid.*, p. 10.

12. Ryan Weddle, "What's Next for the 'F' Process," March 30, 2009, available from *www.devex.com/articles/what-s-next-for-the-f-process*.

13. *Quadrennial Diplomacy and Development Review*, Washington, DC: Department of State, July 10, 2009, available from *www.state.gov/r/pa/prs/ps/2009/july/125956.htm*.

14. *Ibid.*

15. Testimony before the Senate Committee on Foreign Relations, December 1, 2009, available from *www.usaid.gov/press/releases/2009/pr091201.html*.

16. "The Vanguard," available from *www.afsa.org/usaid/0410vanguard.pdf*.

17. U.S. Department of State, available from *www.state.gov/secretary/rm/2009a/01/115297.htm*.

18. *Transparency International Corruption Perceptions Index 2009*, available from *www.transparency.org/policy_research/surveys_indices/cpi/2009/cpi_2009_table*.

19. Major Paul P. Cale, "The United States Military Advisory Group In El Salvador, 1979-1992," p. 13, *available from smallwarsjournal.com/documents/cale.pdf*.

20. *Ibid.*, p. 14.

CHAPTER 9

OUR STRATEGIC ASSESSMENT "SYSTEM"
NEEDS AN OVERHAUL:
SUMMARY AND CONCLUDING THOUGHTS

Matthew Harber

Throughout this book, all the authors in one form or another have provided insight into a midterm assessment of the Obama administration. The strength of all the contributed articles is the scope of subjects that were covered. These subjects included how the U.S. national security system needs reform and the best possible ways to go about this, highlighting the need for Congress to take most of the initiative. Additional topics included the U.S. handling of the Iraq and Afghanistan invasions and the future of U.S. stabilization and reconstruction efforts. In this chapter, each preceeding chapter will be reviewed, engaging in a discussion of what should be expected of President Obama and U.S. foreign policy in the last 2 years of his first term regarding national security reform.

In Chapter 2, James Carafano includes a dual argument: (1) that through proposed defense spending cuts the United States is putting itself at risk from international security threats; and (2) that whole-of-government approaches are quite possible but difficult within our governmental structure. Carafano postulates that these problems are causing the key instruments of the American national security system to fall into neutral. Furthermore, if these issues are not addressed, then one could actually see the American national security system regress and put the country at large at risk.

Carafano vehemently argues against defense spending cuts as a method for politicians to make simple pronouncements. He counters one of the traditional claims—that if only Washington could cut down on military spending, America's fiscal issues would be solved. He points out that defense spending ranks fourth in the overall federal budget; it trails financial support for the elderly, education funding, and means-tested welfare programs. Furthermore, even if Washington were to cut defense spending, this would not have any significant impact on solving the country's budgetary problems. The problem arises when proposals link reductions in defense spending to solving U.S. fiscal issues, while forgetting the international ramifications.

According to Carafano, the American military simply has some missions that if abandoned or compromised, would put the United States at risk. In other words, what the American people expect of the military on an international level simply cannot be done with fewer forces, capabilities, and funding. To put it succinctly, this expectation defies common sense. Rather, for the U.S. military to accomplish the goals expected of it requires predictable levels of spending. Stability in defense spending allows the military to maintain and modernize its arsenals. More importantly, predictable levels of spending would allow the military to train its forces for all types of warfare. This is extremely important, since the threats facing the United States are complex and take on many forms. Therefore, the military must be able and ready to confront any of these potential threats when asked to. Unfortunately, Carafano argues, the U.S. military is not able to be properly prepared, as described above, because policymakers are making the incorrect assumption that potential threats will never emerge. There is the potential that the military will be turned into a "hollow force" that will lack the capabilities necessary to keep the nation free, safe, and prosperous.

The other half of Carafano's argument for strengthening America's national security system is that a whole-of-government approach must be adopted. Carafano argues that this can be accomplished through better congressional oversight and a deeper understanding of the interagency process. The current congressional oversight process, filled with overlapping committees, simply leads to inefficiency and detracts from overall effectiveness. Carafano proposes that the solution to this oversight conundrum is to collapse the multiple committees within the House and Senate into single entities for each legislative chamber. In fact, he argues that such an action should be a top priority. Unfortunately though, neither Congress nor the White House has shown any initiative in instituting such internal reforms.

Additionally, Carafano believes that some policymakers simply do not understand the entire interagency process. This lack of understanding deters from creating a whole-of-government national security system paradigm. Carafano argues that the interagency process can be broken down into three levels: policy, operations, and practice. The level that requires significant attention, scrutiny, and reform is operations. The driving factors behind the operational weakness originate from flaws in the divide between military and civilian circles, including distinct institutional cultures, lack of trust between actors within the interagency process, and lack of interagency operational experience. Until those issues are addressed, the operational level will remain weak. In Carafano's view Congress and the White House, the two agents most capable of stimulating effective and efficient interagency operations, have not shown enough interest or committed enough resources to overcoming these obstacles. Therefore, real national security reform must start with Congress; Congress can create a legislative framework in which federal agencies can be staffed with responsible people who are skilled in the interagency process.

In Chapter 3, Dr. Bernard Finel critically challenges the whole-of-government approach that revolves around better integration of the various instruments of statecraft as well as better training and education for a cadre of national security specialists. Finel believes that this is such a big subject of debate within national security reform, because for some reason policymakers assume that it is in America's interest to maintain a "quasi-colonial" presence overseas. Finel argues that this assumption needs to be challenged and examined in far more detail. Specifically, policymakers must be able to admit that it might not be in America's interest to be so involved internationally. Finel believes that there must be national security reform, but it must revolve around introducing disciplined cost-benefit analyses to involvement in particular conflicts, improving civil-military relations, and imposing checks on any sort of unlawful activity.

Dr. Finel does agree that conflicts in today's world are becoming more complex, complicated, interconnected, and confusing to understand. However, it is because of these various components that policymakers absolutely must utilize improved cost-benefit analyses. The purpose of these analyses is to determine up front whether the United States has the available resources and that the benefits are tangible if the United

States does decide to commit itself to any particular conflict. For if the United States fails to do strict cost-benefit analysis, it could commit itself to a conflict in which it will incur more costs then benefits, thus not serving U.S. interests. Logically, the United States should make these assessments before committing military forces. Finel, therefore, recommends that national security expenditures follow the congressional PAYGO rule, which stresses budget neutrality. That is, any expenditure must be offset with revenue increases or spending cuts. This would start the U.S. national security system down a path of cost-effectiveness and meaningful strategic and operational assessments.

As for improving civil-military relations, Finel proposes three major changes: (1) insulate the Chairman of the Joint Chiefs of Staff (CJCS) from political pressures, (2) ban general officers (except for the CJCS) from any public statements, and (3) impose regulations on the tapping of recently retired officers as political appointees.

In general, the Chairman of the Joint Chiefs of Staff must be able to provide candid advice to the President and Congress about military issues. In the current system, the Chairman is unable to do that. Therefore, the benefits of insulating him from political pressures become readily apparent. First and foremost, it will allow him to provide the President the best possible military advice, allowing the President to make the best decision. Also, by being above political pressures, the CJCS can act as a conduit for military dissent. By having the CJCS fulfill this function, Finel hopes to also limit the number of military leaks and back-channel military lobbying.

Dr. Finel also argues that general officers must see their profiles diminish. In other words, they must believe they have to take it upon themselves not to break with the chain of command by publicly disagreeing with a policy decision and not to resort to back-channel lobbying. The main negative consequence that occurs when such an event happens is that it sends mixed signals of a lack of cohesiveness between the military and civilian government to the international community. This can have significant consequences internationally, and particularly in how U.S. policies are received abroad. Therefore, according to Finel, all general officers except for the Chairman should be banned from giving public statements. This includes speeches to think tanks, universities, newspapers, and television stations.

According to Finel, there has been a steady increase in recently retired officers being tapped to serve as political appointees. The major risks of this policy are that it runs the possibility of politicizing the military and eroding professionalism in the officer corps. In other words, the tapping of retired officers as political appointees may weaken the ability of our officers to provide the strictly military advice required of them. To avoid such a situation, Finel proposes that there should be strict regulation regarding this. Specifically, there must be a 5-year period after retirement before a retired officer may be tapped as a political appointee. Also, no serving general should be eligible to run any government agency.

The third dimension of Finel's approach to national security reform is to impose checks on any unlawful activity. He argues that over the past decade, the U.S. national security community has been implicated in various unlawful activities such as war crimes (and their cover-up), unlawful domestic surveillance, and torture. One of the first steps needed to limit such activities is to clarify personal liability. Second, there needs to be some form of independent authority that has the jurisdiction to investigate and initiate criminal proceedings into allegations of unlawful activities. If all three areas are addressed, then the United States will have achieved meaningful national security reform in the eyes of Finel.

In Chapter 4, Jim Locher argues that national security reform is the responsibility of Congress. According to Locher, Congress can spearhead reform through its oversight of the application, administration, and execution of its laws. Locher argues that there is a precedent for Congress-driven reform in the national security community with the 1986 Goldwater-Nichols Act. As such, any argument that such reform cannot be done is wrong, because large-scale reform has been implemented before through legislative initiatives.

Locher argues that the current national security system is not suited to handle the immediate threat environment. Rather, the current system is a legacy of the post-World War II environment, in which stove-piped agencies and departments were responsible for implementing the instruments of national power. Some argue that there was only a limited need for extensive interagency cooperation during the Cold War. However, in today's environment, interagency cooperation is the name of the game; because of the stove-pipe legacy, Congress is actually reinforcing divisions in the executive branch while magnifying interagency gaps and cleavages. According to Locher, Congress must become more relevant in national security issues by legislating and overseeing methods of promoting interagency cooperation.

Proponents of Congress should not despair. Locher argues that Congress is taking an active interest in national security reform by promoting efficiency,

economy, effectiveness, responsiveness, and accountability among federal departments. Unfortunately,
whatever reform that has been accomplished has not
been enough to overcome the current interagency
gap. Locher believes this to be the case because, unlike
the Cold War-era Goldwater-Nichols Act, the contemporary security threat environment is far more complex. Modern threats define the three D's paradigm
(diplomacy, development, and defense) and require
more interagency cooperation. In addition, the abso-
lute scope of reform needed today is far greater than
what was needed in 1986. Locher estimates that the
needed size of today's reform is about 15 to 20 times
larger than what was required in 1986. As a direct result of this enormous need, additional agencies will
have to be included within the reform framework, including those generally not associated with national
security. Locher also states that entirely new entities
might need to be created, which was not the case in
the Goldwater-Nichols Act of 1986.

In short, national security reform will require Congress to take the helm. Unfortunately, according to Locher, no single congressional committee sees itself as
having the mandate for initiating such major reform,
thus immediately hindering the reform process. In addition, for significant reform to occur, it must happen
through bipartisan channels. Obviously, today's Congress is characterized by extremely partisan politics.
In short, while Congress does have a precedent for national security reform, there are many obstacles facing
today's reform framework.

In Chapter 5, Dr. Richard Weitz also argues for
national security reform that must come through Congress. Weitz's argument distinguishes itself from those
of the previous authors by calling for the establish-

ment of a *National Security Review,* a *National Security Strategy,* and a *National Security Planning and Resource Guidance* as a set of documents. All these documents will be ordered and approved by the President, thus providing a clear and coherent national security system.

The *National Security Review* would be used to assess strategic challenges and capabilities. This document would describe the strategic landscape and assess existing capabilities and resources against America's strategic needs. The *National Security Review* (NSR) would also make recommendations regarding missions, activities, and budgets. Most importantly, the NSR would review the scope and assumptions of national security, especially related to the changes in roles and responsibilities of those within the interagency process.

The *National Security Review* would also be used to create the *National Security Strategy.* The *National Security Planning and Resource Guidance* document would then translate the *National Security Strategy* into policy, planning, and resource guidance to all the relevant departments and agencies, that is, the whole-of-government.

One more distinctive element of Weitz's argument is that the national security system must do a better job of capturing and leveraging data and knowledge. There have been several cases in which important information has been presented to one agency but has failed to make it to other agencies that have a stake in the consequences of that knowledge.

In Chapter 6, Dr. Harvey Sicherman argues that to understand national security reform as well as President Obama's changes to the National Security Council, one has to place them within an historical context.

Since the 1947 National Security Act, intrinsic patterns have emerged. Sicherman offers three examples of functional trends: Truman-Acheson, early Nixon-Kissinger, and Bush-Scowcroft-Baker. Sicherman also offers two dysfunctional trends: Reagan-Haig and later Nixon-Kissinger.

First, it is important to know that the policymakers who promoted a new national security system in the 1940s were men who had experience in preparing the United States for a two-front war. The role of the national security system was to create an organization that provided the President with critical information, competing views and efficient execution. In short, this new organization was intended to provide the President with the means to coordinate action while creating order between the Cabinet and the President.

In the Truman-Acheson framework, President Truman believed that he was accountable to Congress and the American people but not to the National Security Council (NSC). In other words, for Truman, the NSC was an organization to provide advice and information, not dictate direction. Direction came from the President alone, and it was the NSC's responsibility to carry out his policy effectively and efficiently. In subscribing to this noncollegial framework, President Truman believed strongly in Cabinet responsibility. While Sicherman categorizes the Truman-Acheson framework as a functional one, he explicitly states that functionality does not equate to correct decision-making. While the Truman-Acheson framework was extremely successful in producing the containment paradigm and providing effective crisis management during the Korean War, it also experienced failures. For example, Truman's NSC was not prepared for the military gap when North Korea invaded South Korea. Also, Truman's NSC approved General Douglas

McArthur's post-Inchon offensive, which brought China into the war.

The dysfunctional counterpart to the Truman-Acheson framework is that of Reagan-Haig. The dysfunctionality of this framework came from having a national security system that was at odds with President Ronald Reagan's personality. Reagan believed in Cabinet consensus, especially on issues that he lacked knowledge about, or those that he did not have any serious convictions. What resulted from this emphasis on consensus was a "ghost ship" national security system. In other words, no one knew what was wanted or expected from the President. As a result, this left the NSC rudderless and uncertain of what direction the White House desired.

Dr. Sicherman claims that the most recent example of a functional and effective NSC framework is that of Bush-Scowcroft-Baker. According to Sicherman, when Bush, Scowcroft, and Baker took office, they were appalled by the Reagan national security system, mostly because they saw the NSC as extremely defective. The national security framework under President Bush was one that was similar to the Truman-Acheson framework in that Cabinet responsibility, along with the NSC, was an important concept. The Bush-Scowcroft-Baker approach included an orderly process within the NSC that ultimately gave everyone a role and a stake. Additionally, under the Bush-Scowcroft-Baker framework, the NSC was extremely disciplined, which helped U.S. diplomacy, since Washington sent few mixed signals internationally.

Dr. Sicherman argues that the Bush-Scowcroft-Baker and Truman-Acheson frameworks demonstrate that when it comes to national security, the integrity of the process is an important factor. That is, the process matters: It is fair, talent is concentrated, and decisions are implemented effectively. When the policy process is appreciated and properly followed, one can have an effective and efficient national security system. Sicherman claims that President Obama's NSC is a hybrid one that tries to revolve around the Bush-Scowcroft-Baker framework. The NSC advisor and staff are expected to function as advisors and facilitators, but there are still many important functions that the White House feels that it is completely responsible for carrying out. However, it seems that President Obama highly values consensus, similarly to Reagan, and this has caused problems, according to Sicherman. First, leaks have been a very large problem within the Obama administration. This is undermining the Obama-Biden framework, since the leaks weaken the appearance of a unified national security system. Also, Sicherman argues that the compromises within the Obama-Biden framework are negatively affecting the implementation of the national security system in the field.

Based on his analytical case studies of various national security approaches, Sicherman identifies three major points: First, Presidents must choose their system. Second, integrity is extremely important as it will determine how effective one's framework is. Third, strategy counts.

In Chapter 7, Joseph Collins provides a perspective on nonlinear change within Afghanistan. Collins argues that change in Afghanistan will be driven by the intersection of five vectors. The first vector is that U.S. objectives are and will remain the guide for policies and strategies. The second vector is that the costs of the Afghan War, in any way that one may look at it, are extremely high. For example, Afghanistan has consistently been at war for over 30 years. Also, the amount of causalities is staggering: 1,000 American soldiers dead, 10,000 Pakistani soldiers dead, and tens of thousands of dead Afghans. The third vector within Afghanistan is that the Taliban are now beginning to feel the pressure of Obama's surge. The fourth vector is that President Karzai's government is weak, corrupt, ineffective, and thus, unfortunately, has become the Taliban's ultimate talking point for recruiting. The fifth and final vector is that the Afghan people are sick of war and are tired of the presence of coalition forces. Fortunately for the coalition forces, the Afghan people despise the Taliban more than their own government and its coalition partners. In short, these vectors have created a situation in which nonlinear change is highly possible.

Collins points out that while U.S. forces did not completely destroy the enemy or its will and ability to resist, there were significant improvements in other areas within Afghanistan. First, under Finance Minister Ashraf Ghani, a single stable currency was created out of several viral currencies. Second, health-care access increased from 15 percent to 85 percent of the total Afghan population. While these were significant improvements, there was limited nation-building expectation, as Afghan good governance was not a priority within the Bush administration. Collins goes on to argue that this would have significant implications during the latter years of the Afghan war. More specifically, it would cause the war in Afghanistan to go from a highlight in the Global War on Terrorism, to a highly controversial issue in terms of the U.S. Government's nation-building role.

One of the direct consequences of a limited focus on nation building is that hardly any Afghan governing capacity was created. Due to this lack of capacity and government corruption, much of the international assistance work in Afghanistan was being conducted through nongovernmental organizations (NGOs) and foreign contractors. As such, the Afghan government had little control over what was going on, but more significantly, it was not learning how to be self-sufficient and sustainable. A negative spillover effect of this was that the Afghan government lost key ministers who had great potential. In addition, the capacity of the Afghan security forces, especially the police, failed to materialize. This happened because coalition arms, aid, trainers, and advisors ended up being either too little, too slow, or too inefficient.

As the security situation continued to deteriorate within Afghanistan, a new military paradigm was recommended by General Stanley McChrystal: a population-centric counterinsurgency strategy. An important recommendation within this new strategy was the emphasis on greater partnering between U.S. and Afghan forces, increasing the size of the Afghan national security forces, improving Afghan governance, and gaining the initiative from the Taliban. In response, President Obama committed an additional 30,000 troops to Afghanistan, with the stipulation that the United States would not tolerate an open-ended commitment and that by July 2011, American troops would begin to leave Afghanistan.

In December 2010, the United States will re-evaluate its commitment to Afghanistan. Collins argues that three options will be dominant in the minds of key policymakers. First, the United States could continue its current strategy of a population-centric counterinsurgency strategy, with troop levels remaining where they are. While this option would facilitate building

Afghan capacity, it would be expensive for the United States. Additionally, it would provide the Taliban with a recruiting platform of the coalition being an occupying force.

Second, the United States could reduce most of the 30,000 Soldiers and Marines associated with President Obama's surge over the period of a year. While this is going on, the priority of the International Security Assistance Forces would be to prioritize and focus on security assistance and capacity building. This option would also be expensive, but it would allow for American troops to return home. However, as American forces are replaced with Afghan ones, there could be temporary short-term security problems. Collins argues that this could be particularly problematic for negotiations within Afghanistan.

Third, Collins posits that the Afghan government, along with United Nations (UN) and coalition support, could work toward reintegration and reconciliation with parts or the entirety of the Afghan Taliban. Collins argues that if this approach is adopted, there needs to be strict limits on the reintegration and reconciliation process. First, war criminals should not be involved this process. Also, the Afghan constitution cannot be bargained away, and all participants must renounce violence and al Qaeda. The potential drawbacks of this option, according to Collins, are that it could provide the Taliban with an opportunity to negotiate and fight simultaneously. Collins, however, it is imperative that the United States does not stand in the way of reconciliation with the Taliban.

Change will of course be nonlinear in Afghanistan, and there are key issues that the United States can tackle to help influence the outcome. First, it is imperative that the United States maintain pressure on the Taliban. Second, it is crucial that the United States focus on building Afghanistan's governance capacity, not just in security areas, but in civil government and the private sectors as well. In short, for Collins, change in Afghanistan will depend on how all these issues are dealt with systematically and how each of the five vectors interact with each other.

Finally, in Chapter 8, James Stephenson provides a detailed case study of U.S. stabilization and reconstruction efforts in Iraq and Afghanistan. In addition, he provides what he believes is the path for more effective stabilization and reconstruction operations. Initially, U.S. Secretary of Defense Donald Rumsfeld did not want to focus on post-war reconstruction in Iraq. However, after the 2003 invasion, Rumsfeld changed his mind and insisted that the Department of Defense (DoD) assume responsibility for post-war reconstruction. According to Stephenson, Rumsfeld changed his mind, not because of a fundamental change of heart, but because the budgets for the Department of State and the U.S. Agency for International Development (USAID) were relatively small compared to the DoD budget. To carry out post-war reconstruction in Iraq, the DoD created the Office of Reconstruction and Humanitarian Assistance (OHRA). However, the OHRA had barely reached Baghdad, before the DoD informed it that the agency had been dissolved. In its place, the Coalition Provisional Authority (CPA) was created, with a mission statement of rebuilding the infrastructure of Iraq.

However, according to Stephenson, the CPA never had a coherent strategy for rebuilding Iraq. Stephenson's main argument is that the principle strategy flaw of the CPA was that it tried to do everything at once instead of choosing to focus on specific sectors. The CPA received an $18.4 billion budget, which completely focused on large infrastructure projects. Stephenson argues that the problem with such a heavy focus on infrastructure in a post-conflict country is that it fails to produce immediate benefits that allow locals to see their lives improving. Additionally, the CPA was staffed with temporary hires who generally had little to no experience with stabilization and reconstruction projects. As a result, the CPA also suffered from a lack of ability to implement its strategy. As such, Stephenson believes the CPA in Iraq was doomed from the start.

According to Stephenson, what the DoD and the CPA failed to realize was the intricate relationship between stabilization and reconstruction. Stabilization enables the necessary governance, security, and economic activity that allows the process of reconstruction of civil society, governance, security, and the economy. In Afghanistan, USAID and State failed dramatically, because they focused on a top-down approach. In other words, they tried to create a government in a country that for decades never knew what governance even meant. Additionally, the U.S. efforts at stabilization and reconstruction failed within Afghanistan because they were Kabul-centric and, as result, a majority of Afghans were completely oblivious to any efforts made to improve their lives.

As opposed to the failed or poorly implemented stabilization and reconstructions efforts undertaken by the United States in Afghanistan and Iraq, Stephenson proposes a leaner and more sustainable model. In proposing this model, he draws on what he calls a successful counterinsurgency program in El Salvador. The main takeaway from El Salvador, according to Stephenson, is that since the United States was unable to go big (compared to the CPA), the United States was forced to invest time, intelligence, equipment, and training to enable the El Salvadorian armed forces to defeat the insurgents instead of doing it for them. While this military capacity was being built, complimentary investments were being made by US-AID in improving the conditions that had initially led to the insurgency. What El Salvador can teach those interested in stabilization and reconstruction is that success at post-conflict transition is predicated on the right enabling strategy and on implementation by experienced practitioners with both time and patience. On the other hand, a bad strategy is a bad strategy, and no amount of extra money will fix it.

Considering the contributions of all the authors, there are a some major takeaways: First, national security reform must be driven by Congress. Second, strategic planning and assessment must be done around a whole-of-government approach, while being fiscally responsible and incorporating a transition of power to civilian leadership.

Congress-driven reform must focus on better efficiency, oversight and interagency cooperation. The need for efficiency in establishing a new national security framework is that it will allow a baseline budget to be established. By providing a clear baseline, it will remove the constant state of suspense and uncertainty from those who are involved in the national security system. That is, they will know what kind of resources they have at their disposal. For example, defense spending should be based on a 3- to 6-year schedule, since this will provide the defense community with the time to adjust to whatever challenges arise.

In pursuing better oversight, Congress can improve the interagency process. Proper oversight from Congress will allow each federal agency involved in national security to know exactly what its proper functions and jurisdictions are. In addition, oversight will allow for the interagency process to coordinate strategy across the three D's: defense, diplomacy, and development. This area of reform should be put to the top of the list, as our authors have clearly argued that a functional interagency process is critical for the national security system. However, this process needs to be pursued in a continually incremental way. This will allow the national security system to adapt to the environment facing it. More importantly, to make this work, Congress must leverage the correct personnel. With the right people in place, the interagency process can work properly and achieve the goals handed down to it by Congress.

Our second major takeaway is that strategic planning and assessments must adopt a whole-of-government approach. This must happen in a fiscally responsible way, while ensuring the transition of power to civilian leadership in Iraq and Afghanistan. A whole-of-government approach will allow the national security community to position itself to be capable of handling the next critical situation. Currently, we are operating under the assumption that Iraq and Afghanistan are the last wars that will be fought by the United States. Such an assumption is not only incorrect, but it places the United States in a vulnerable position. With the complexities of threats facing the United States, the national security system must be prepared to respond to each one on an appropriate, efficient, and effective scale.

ABOUT THE CONTRIBUTORS

JARED "ETHAN" BENNETT graduated cum laude from the University of Kentucky in December 2005 with a B.A. in Spanish, international economics and Latin American studies. He earned the distinction of honors in the Department of Hispanic Studies and was inducted into five honor societies, among them Golden Key International Honour Society, where he was elected vice president. Mr. Bennett was also awarded the University of Kentucky Arts and Sciences Merit Scholarship for his scholastic achievement. He served twice in Chile as part of the United Nations sponsored program "English Opens Doors." This program, aimed at teaching English to Chilean youth, was operated through the Chilean Ministry of Education in the towns of Quilpué and Valparaíso. Mr. Bennett graduated from the Bush School of Government and Public Service at Texas A&M University in 2010.

JOSEPH R. CERAMI is a Professor at the Bush School of Government and Public Service at Texas A&M University, where he teaches courses on Leadership and National Security Policy. He also serves as the current Director of the Bush School's Public Service Leadership Program. Dr. Cerami is a distinguished scholar, having co-edited multiple Strategic Studies Institute publications.

ROBERT "ROBIN" DORFF joined the Strategic Studies Institute as a Research Professor of National Security Affairs in June 2007. Dr. Dorff remains extensively involved in strategic leadership development, focusing on national security strategy and policy, and on strategy formulation. His research interests include failing and fragile states, interagency processes and U.S. grand strategy.

JAMES CARAFANO currently serves as the Deputy Director at the Kathryn and Shelby Cullom Davis Institute for International Studies. He is also the Director of the Douglas and Sarah Allison Center for Foreign Policy Studies. Dr. Carafano works with the Heritage Foundation, where he focuses on developing national security policies required to secure the long-term interests of the United States.

JOSEPH COLLINS is a Professor at the National War College, where he teaches national security strategy. Dr. Collins has served as the Deputy Assistant Secretary of Defense for Stability Operations. His team led the stability operations effort in Afghanistan. Dr. Collins was also a Senior Fellow at the Center for Strategic and International Studies.

PATRICK CRONIN is a Senior Advisor and Senior Director of the Asia-Pacific Security Program at the Center for a New American Security. Prior to his current position, he was the Director of the Institute for National Strategic Studies at the National Defense University. Dr. Cronin had 25 years of experience in government and academic research centers, in which he dealt with such issues as defense affairs, foreign policy, and development assistance.

SCOTT R. FEIL is a retired U.S. Army colonel who serves as an Adjunct Research Staff Member in the Operation Evaluation Division at the Institute for Defense Analyses. He has also served as the Executive Director of the Program on the Role of American

Military Power and as co-director on a project on Post-Conflict Reconstruction.

BERNARD I. FINEL is a Senior Fellow at the American Security Project, where he directs research on "Securing America in an Age of Terror." Dr. Finel is the lead author of the American Security Project's annual report, "Are We Winning? Measuring Progress in the Struggle against Violent Jihadism." He also produces in-depth analyses on the developments in the wars in Iraq and Afghanistan and on U.S. defense policy.

MATTHEW HARBER graduated cum laude from Truman State University (MO) with a B.A. in political science and history. In the summer of 2008 he was one of eight undergraduates who attended the Research Experience for Undergraduates (REU) at Oklahoma State University. There he wrote a research paper that he later presented at the International Studies Association (ISA) conference in New York. He also presented a second research paper at the student conferences at both Illinois State University and Truman State University. Mr. Harber is a member of Pi Sigma Alpha (national political science honor society) and has lived abroad in Zambia, Madagascar, South Africa, Mozambique, Egypt, and Uganda. He is a 2011 graduate of the Bush School of Government and Public Service at Texas A&M University.

JAMES M. LINDSAY is the Senior Vice President, Director of Studies, and Maurice R. Greenberg Chair at the Council on Foreign Relations. He is considered a leading authority on the American foreign policy-making process and the domestic politics of American foreign policy. Dr. Lindsay has also served as the director of the Robert S. Strauss Center for International Security and Law at the University of Texas at Austin.

JAMES R. LOCHER III is currently the President and CEO of the Project on National Security Reform. He has more than 25 years of professional experience in both the executive and legislative branches of the federal government, including service as the chairman of the Defense Reform Commission of Bosnia and Herzegovina.

THOMAS G. MAHNKEN has served as the Deputy Assistant Secretary of Defense for Policy Planning since November 2006. He is responsible for the major strategic planning function within the Office of the Secretary of Defense. Dr. Mahnken also served as the Deputy Assistant Secretary of Defense for Resources and Plans and the Acting Deputy Assistant Secretary of Defense for Policy Planning.

DONALD L. "LARRY" SAMPLER, JR., is the Vice President and Director of the Communities in Transition division of Creative Associates, International. His division focuses on societies recovering from trauma and works alongside civilian and military actors, international partners, and host-nation civil society and governments. Mr. Sampler previously served as the Deputy Coordinator for Reconstruction and Stabilization.

NINA SERAFINO is a Specialist in International Security Affairs at the Congressional Research Service Foreign Affairs, Defense, and Trade Division. Previously she worked on Latin American issues, including the Central American wars and peace processes, and U.S. policy toward Colombia.

HARVEY SICHERMAN was the President and Director of the Foreign Policy Research Institute in Pennsylvania. He had extensive experiencing working in government. Dr. Sicherman served under Secretary of State Alexander M. Haig, Jr., and Secretary of State James A. Baker III; and acted as a consultant to Secretary of the Navy John F. Lehman, Jr. and Secretary of State George Shultz.

JAMES "SPIKE" STEPHENSON is the Senior Advisor for Stabilization and Reconstruction at Creative Associates International, Inc. He is a retired Senior Foreign Service Officer with the U.S. Agency for International Development. His duties included being the Mission Director in Iraq and Senior Advisor to the State Department's Coordinator for Reconstruction and Stabilization.

BETH TRITTER is a Managing Director at the Glover Park Group and specializes in government relations and strategic communications. She has focused primarily on clients with an interest in U.S. foreign policy. Ms. Tritter has advised multinational corporations such as Standard Charted Bank and De Beers on leadership strategies. She has worked for nearly a decade on Capitol Hill as Legislative Director for Congresswoman Nita Lowey of New York.

RICHARD WEITZ is a Senior Fellow and Director of the Center for Political-Military Analysis at the Hudson Institute. His research interests include regional security developments relating to Europe, Eurasia, and East Asia, as well as U.S. foreign, defense, homeland security, and weapons of mass destruction nonproliferation policies. Dr. Weitz is also a non-resident Senior Fellow at the Project on National Security Reform as well as the Center for a New American Security.

THE BUSH SCHOOL OF GOVERNMENT
AND PUBLIC SERVICE

The Bush School of Government and Public Service at Texas A&M University is located in College Station, Texas. Established in 1997, the Bush School was created to honor the vision of its founder, George H. W. Bush, the 41st President of the United States. At the groundbreaking of the compound, President Bush shared his conviction that working for government, whether as an elected official or civil servant, should be viewed as dedication to public service:

> I want to share with the students my thoughts on public service—that service to a country is a calling and that . . . in a far broader sense it means helping others and sacrificing and contributing to causes bigger than yourself.

The Bush School is dedicated to academic integrity, leadership development, professional experience, and unique relationships between professors and students academically and in research. In the Bush School, there are two distinct master degrees: The **Master of Public Service & Administration (MPSA)** and the **Master's Program in International Affairs (MPIA)**. The MPSA program focuses on public management and public policy analysis and offers five areas of concentration, including nonprofit management; state/local policy and management; energy, environment, and technology policy and management; security policy and management; health policy and management; and individually created options. The MPIA program focuses on international economics and development and on national security and diplomacy. It has nine concentrations, including American diplomacy, intelligence as statecraft, defense policy and military affairs, international politics, homeland security, regional studies (Europe, Middle East, and China), international economics, international economic development, and multinational enterprises and public policy. The Bush School program also offers students opportunities at national and international internships, and emphasizes the development of written and oral communication skills. For the past decade, the Bush School has prepared leaders who can share the work of public service with a diversified set of players—both in and out of government. Its graduates have quickly established themselves in exciting careers in government, nonprofits, international organizations, think tanks, international financial institutions, and businesses; the School will continue to graduate students who make a difference.

The Bush School, along with the Strategic Studies Institute, is proud to put forward this book, both institutes believe the individual opinions expressed within are valuable and important.

THE STRATEGIC STUDIES INSTITUTE

The Strategic Studies Institute (SSI) is the U.S. Army's center for geostrategic and national security research and analysis. SSI conducts strategic research and analysis to support the U.S. Army War College (USAWC) curriculum, provides direct analysis for Army and Department of Defense (DoD) leadership, and serves as a bridge to the wider strategic community.

SSI is composed of civilian research professors, uniformed military officers, and a professional support staff. All have extensive credentials and experience. SSI is divided into four components: the Strategic Research and Analysis Department focuses on global, transregional, and functional issues, particularly those dealing with Army transformation; the Regional Strategy Department focuses on regional strategic issues; the Academic Engagement Program creates and sustains partnerships with the global strategic community; and the Publications Department maintains a web of partnerships with strategic analysts around the world, including the foremost thinkers in the fields of security and military strategy. In most years, about half of SSI's publications are written by these external partners.

SSI documents are published by the Institute and distributed to key strategic leaders in the Army and the DoD, the military educational system, Congress, the news media, other think tanks and defense institutes, and major colleges and universities. SSI publications use history and current political, economic, and military factors to develop strategic recommendations.

SSI has a variety of publications, including:

- Books - SSI publishes about 3-5 books per year consisting of authored works or edited compilations.
- Monographs – Policy-oriented reports provide recommendations. They are usually 25-90 pages in length.
- Carlisle Papers - The best of the student papers submitted in compliance with requirements for graduation from the USAWC are highlighted.
- LeTort Papers - Essays, retrospectives, or speeches of interest to the defense academic community.
- Colloquium Reports - For larger conferences, SSI may produce a report on the proceedings.
- Colloquium Briefs - These 2- to 4-page briefs are produced after the colloquia that SSI has co-sponsored or helped to fund.

At the request of the Army leadership, SSI sometimes provides shorter analytical reports on pressing strategic issues. The distribution of these is usually limited.

Additionally, every year SSI compiles a Key Strategic Issues List (KSIL) based on input from the USAWC faculty, the Army Staff, the Joint Staff, the unified and specified commands, and other Army organizations. This is designed to guide the research of SSI, the USAWC, and other Army-related strategic analysts.

SSI analysts publish widely outside of the Institute's own products. They have written books for Cambridge University Press, Princeton University Press, University Press of Kansas, Duke University Press, Praeger, Frank Cass, Rowman and Littlefield, and Brassey's. They have contributed chapters to many other books, including publications from the Brookings Institution, Jane's Defense Group, and the Center for Strategic and International Studies. SSI analysts have written articles for more than 50 journals and periodicals on history, strategy, national security, and a myriad of other relevant topics.

SSI also co-sponsors academic conferences to examine issues of importance to the Army, collaborating with some of the leading universities in the country. Recent partners have included Georgetown, Princeton, Harvard, MIT, Columbia, University of Chicago, University of Miami, Stanford, Georgia Tech, Johns Hopkins, and the Bush School of Government and Public Service at Texas A&M University.

U.S. ARMY WAR COLLEGE

Major General Gregg F. Martin
Commandant

*****

STRATEGIC STUDIES INSTITUTE

Director
Professor Douglas C. Lovelace, Jr.

Director of Research
Dr. Antulio J. Echevarria II

Editors
Dr. Joseph R. Cerami
Dr. Robert H. Dorff
Dr. Matthew H. Harber

Director of Publications
Dr. James G. Pierce

Publications Assistant
Ms. Rita A. Rummel

*****

Composition
Mrs. Jennifer E. Nevil

www.ingramcontent.com/pod-product-compliance
Lightning Source LLC
Chambersburg PA
CBHW081359270326
41930CB00015B/3358